Books be returned on or before date below.

D1765887

FUNDAMENTALS
OF FORENSIC
ANTHROPOLOGY

Foundations of Human Biology

Series Editors

Matt Cartmill
Kaye Brown
Department of Biological Anthropology and Anatomy
Duke University Medical Center
Durham, North Carolina

The Growth of Humanity, by *Barry Bogin*
Fundamentals of Forensic Anthropology, by *Linda L. Klepinger*

FUNDAMENTALS OF FORENSIC ANTHROPOLOGY

LINDA L. KLEPINGER
Department of Anthropology
University of Illinois at Urbana-Champaign
Urbana, Illinois

A JOHN WILEY & SONS, INC., PUBLICATION

Library of Congress Cataloging-in-Publication Data is available:

Klepinger, Linda L.
  Fundamentals of Forensic Anthropology

ISBN 13: 978-0471-21006-1
ISBN 10: 0-471-21006-4

Printed in the United States of America

10 9 8 7 6 5 4 3 2

CONTENTS

PHOTO CREDITS

The photo figures listed below are courtesy of the following offices and individuals.

Figure 3.1	Bruce Ramseyer
Figures 4.2 and 4.3	Bruce Ramseyer
Figures 6.4, 6.5, 6.6, 6.7 and 6.8	Bruce Ramseyer
Figures 8.1 and 8.2	Kris Bolt
Figure 9.1	Kris Bolt
Figure 9.4	Peoria County Coroner's Office
Figure 9.6	Joe Siefferman
Figure 9.7	Kris Bolt
Figure 10.1	John Heidingsfelder
Figure 10.2	Bruce Ramseyer
Figure 10.3	R. Barry Lewis
Figure 10.4	Bruce Ramseyer
Figure 10.6*a*	John Moore
Figure 10.6*b*	Eldon Quick

ACKNOWLEDGMENTS

The great American tennis champion Althea Gibson (1927–2003) remarked that "No matter what accomplishments you make, somebody helps you." Somebodies, actually.

First and foremost is my colleague Eugene Giles who has, at numerous and various times, acted as sounding board, source man, and diplomatic critic—all with his usual aplomb and attention to detail. Matt Cartmill and Kaye Brown, series editors, were a source of advice and encouragement. Steve Holland's experience in graphics production and publishing was very helpful in getting figures modified and into the proper format.

Several members of the medical–legal community and law enforcement professionals have served as examples of the highest integrity and work ethics in death investigation and tempered my too frequent tendency to cynicism. They are proof that we can and do make a difference. You know who you are. Many thanks.

SERIES INTRODUCTION

The core focus of physical anthropology as a discipline is the biology of human beings in a cultural context. The subfield of forensic anthropology adapts this focus to the special job of identifying unknown remains and seeking and interpreting any evidence relating to the death that the remains may hold. We believe that Linda Klepinger's book will become the classic text in this subfield. *Fundamentals of Forensic Anthropology* embodies a genuine scientific passion for the subject matter, communicated not only through the author's unique critical and evaluative approach to the tools and techniques used in forensic investigations but also through her craft and artistry as a writer.

Forensic anthropologists need to know a great deal about human osteology, skeletal biology, dental anthropology, taphonomy, archeology, genomics, and scientific inquiry in general. Fortunately for us, Klepinger knows all this and more. Best of all, she has the rare gift of being able to take others along with her for an eye-popping ride without demanding that they be similarly knowledgeable. In a prose style both engaging and straightforward, she unveils the history, limitations, accuracies, imprecisions, and future of forensic anthropology. Her book will lead its readers to ask all manner of related questions regarding the science behind forensic techniques, because it will teach them not how to do forensic science but how to think about doing it. This, we believe, is the essence of a classic text.

In this book, professional forensic anthropologists will find guides to help them in estimating from unknown remains an individual's probable age, sex, race and stature. Novices will learn to understand—and question—the science behind such estimates. And everybody who reads this book will discover how much they care about this field, and how important it is that it be done with both authority and honesty. This reflects the field's social significance as well as its intrinsic scientific interest; but most of all, it reflects Klepinger's consummate skill in telling the story of her discipline.

Forensics should be an objective scientific inquiry, not a body of opinion in service to a particular employer. Throughout her career, Linda Klepinger has pursued this ideal with wit, charm, and a tenacious and courageous devotion to the scientific method. Her impatience with less conscientious practitioners is expressed in her comment that the false certainty they profess to offer is perhaps "... best left to those who wear a pointy hat with stars on it." After reading *Fundamentals of Forensic Anthropology*, you will understand why the author quotes Voltaire's aphorism: "Doubt is not a pleasant condition, but certainty is an absurd one."

In editing *Foundations of Human Biology*, we seek to offer students the works of physical anthropology's leading practitioners and its best authors. We are grateful to Linda Klepinger for contributing a work that captures the enthusiasm of crime-scene investigations and channels that enthusiasm into a critical concern for the scientific basis of the investigators' knowledge. Her integration of empirical inquiry, social insight, scientific integrity, and narrative skill exemplifies and carries forward the best traditions of anthropological science.

Kaye Brown
Matt Cartmill

Durham, North Carolina
March 27, 2006

PART I

BACKGROUND SETTING FOR FORENSIC ANTHROPOLOGY

1

INTRODUCTION

There does not exist a category of science to which one can give the name applied science. There are science and the applications of science, bound together as the fruit of the tree which bears it.

—Louis Pasteur

OVERVIEW OF THE FIELD

Pasteur's observation on science appears particularly appropriate to forensic anthropology. The American Board of Forensic Anthropology offers the following definition:

Forensic anthropology is the application of the science of physical anthropology to the legal process. The identification of skeletal, badly decomposed, or otherwise unidentified human remains is important for both legal and humanitarian reasons. Forensic anthropologists apply standard scientific techniques developed in physical anthropology to identify human remains, and to assist in the detection of crime. Forensic anthropologists frequently work in conjunction with forensic pathologists, odontologists, and homicide investigators to identify a decedent, discover evidence of foul play, and/or the postmortem interval. In addition to assisting in locating and recovering suspicious remains, forensic anthropologists work to suggest the age, sex, ancestry, stature, and unique features of a decedent from the skeleton.

Fundamentals of Forensic Anthropology, by Linda L. Klepinger
Copyright © 2006 John Wiley & Sons, Inc.

The roots of forensic anthropology are firmly planted in the twentieth-century academic research of physical (i.e. biological) anthropology, especially bioarchaeology. The quest for extracting the maximum information from skeletal remains of past peoples pushed the envelope of osteology beyond the parameters of study routinely addressed by physicians and anatomists. The knowledge, skills and experience that physical anthropologists focused on to derive biological, and even cultural, information from human skeletons in an archaeological context has proven directly applicable to medical–legal contexts. This is not to state that the research to application flow has been essentially one-way, for that is, indeed, not the case. The growth of research and practice in the forensic realm has created a back-flow of information to bioarchaeological and paleontological endeavors.

Reading the bones for clues to personal identification summed up most of the initial work by anthropologists, who were called upon pretty much on a sporadic, *ad hoc* basis. Increasingly they are called upon to help interpret skeletal evidence with an eye to cause and manner of death. "Simply put, the *cause of death* is any injury or disease that produces a physiological derangement in the body that results in the individual dying" (DiMaio and DiMaio, 1993, p. 3). Therefore, causes of death can be as diverse as gunshot wound, melanoma, or toxic shock. While determinations of causes of death are ultimately the call of pathologists, medical examiners, and coroners, when remains are skeletal, the opinion of the forensic anthropologist counts. However, anthropologists lacking soft tissue evidence must be especially cautious in their pronouncements. For instance, there is no absolute association between linear skull fractures and degree of brain injury, and the cause of death may or may not have any direct connection with a cranial fracture. The *manner of death* is the circumstance that gave rise to the cause of death. In contrast to the myriad possible causes of death, the manner of death has but five categories: natural causes, accident, homicide, suicide, and undetermined. For example, a gunshot wound to the head as a cause of death could result from accidental, homicidal, suicidal, or undetermined circumstances. The circumstances of death are part of the medical–legal investigation that is often amenable to anthropological probing—from assigning manner of death to evaluating the believability of a suspect's account of events.

The *mechanism of death* is the physiological or chemical process, initiated by the cause of death, that leads to the failure of vital organs or organ systems. It is a description of how that bullet to the head or chest eventuated in death. This is not an area of primary concern to the anthropologist and should usually be left to medical personnel.

What is of concern to the anthropologist is maintaining the chain of evidence or chain of custody. The anthropologist must vouch for the security of any remains or other evidence left in his or her custody. The anthropologist must guarantee that the evidence was not tampered with in any undocumented way. Often, but not always, there is a chain of custody form signed and dated in serial fashion by each custodian. In any event, anthropologists should record dates, times, and circumstances of the arrival and departure of evidence and where it was housed in the interim.

Mass disasters and recovery from mass graves present special challenges and obstacles that differ from more typical death investigations in that agencies and command structures, foreign settings, and bureaucracies must be dealt with. Each such instance has its own idiosyncrasies.

Finally, forensic anthropology is very much analogous to clinical practice, especially in regard to decision-making, as described by Dawes *et al.* (1989). We employ both "clinical" judgment, where the practitioner processes information in his or her head, and actuarial judgment, where interpretation is the product of an automatic routine or calculation based on empirically established formulations. The Dawes and co-workers study concluded that in medicine and psychology the actuarially based decisions were superior to the clinically based ones. Their conclusion is of interest to anthropology, but (and this is a very big but) the databases on which their actuarial procedures were based are very much larger than those characteristic of anthropology, and their formulations have been more intensively cross-validated. Discretionary decisions in forensic anthropology retain value and must even be applied to the formulae themselves. The era of autopilot has not yet arrived. Attention must be paid.

EDUCATION AND TRAINING

In the United States and Canada most, but not all, programs in physical anthropology are housed in departments of anthropology. Broad undergraduate training in the four fields of anthropology automatically introduces the student to a broad range of cultural practices and to principles of archaeology. Students should have courses in both field archaeology and in archaeological method and theory. Admission to the Physical Anthropology section of the American Academy of Forensic Sciences requires a masters degree in anthropology, which should reflect an emphasis on physical anthropology, and even more specifically on human osteology/skeletal biology. In practice very few university degrees specify such detail. A Ph.D. in physical anthropology with the same emphasis on some aspect of human osteology is one of the requirements for becoming eligible to sit for the American Board of Forensic Anthropology certifying examination. Galloway and Simmons (1997) present an in-depth look at education in forensic anthropology under changing circumstances.

Forensic anthropology is one of the forensic sciences, and successful practitioners should have the basics of biology, physics, chemistry and mathematics under their belts. These courses teach the student critical thinking
and scientific attitude, and promote efficient interagency and interdisciplin-
ary cooperation. Physical anthropology graduates from departments of
anatomy typically fulfill the natural science basic courses without special
effort, but may need to familiarize themselves with archaeology. A
working knowledge of descriptive and inferential statistics is also essential
for research design and interpretation. Paleopathology and bone histology
are very instructive. Participation in casework and internships is desirable,
but for many universities located outside major urban areas, the opportunities
may be limited.

Quality control in the practice of forensic anthropology has been a
nagging problem. Since there is no such legal infraction as "practicing
anthropology without a license", several *very* lightly trained workers in
aligned areas have been lured into amateur play, much to the detriment of
the field. I do not wish to contribute to this practice of professional crossover,
and I offer this—Warning: *This Book Will NOT Make You an Expert!*

OVERVIEW OF THE BOOK

The emphasis of this book follows the two main subdivisions of forensic
anthropological work: the quest for personal identification from skeletal
remains and the role of the anthropologist in the broader medical–legal
investigation. Although somewhat peripheral to the practice of a majority
of forensic anthropologists, genetics and DNA analysis will be presented in
a very brief overview of the basics of terminology and interpretation that
physical anthropologists need in the forensic science world. Physical anthropologists are already familiar with the basic concepts of both Mendelian
and population genetics. The technologies change, but the principles
remain. The emphasis of this book is the *core knowledge* that one needs to
know in order to practice anthropological forensics; the volume deals only
in passing with the related discipline of taphonomy and not at all with
archaeological survey and excavation. Other special techniques that some
anthropologists practice, such as facial reconstruction and photographic
superimposition, will not be covered in this book.

The targeted audience for this book is advanced undergraduate and graduate students and post-graduates who have familiarity with skeletal anatomy
and some introduction to statistics. Less specifically prepared readers will
find sections of interest and learn of strengths and limitations, but will not
fully benefit from the issues and critiques discussed herein. The aim of the

book is to provide the essential foundation for the practice of forensic anthropology and to serve as a guide to the evaluation and use of the primary literature. The book routinely gives sample sizes (n values) and the demographic breakdown of samples. While this scarcely makes for a page-turner, it does allow the reader to evaluate the bases from which the conclusions were drawn and, therefore, the extent of their valid applicability. The emphasis is on presenting those aspects of skeletal biology that are of most direct use in forensic casework. Potential pitfalls of methods, applications and areas of uncertainty and disagreement are included.

This book is not a compendium of all available charts and regression formulae; it is not a cookbook of pretested recipes for arriving at identifications. Instead, the critical and evaluative approach stresses the cautionary note that the variation inherent in human biology places certain constraints on the techniques of forensic anthropology, especially on the narrowness of confidence intervals and the degrees of certainty. We must remember that, even under ideal circumstances, 95 percent confidence in an answer means error is expected five percent of the time, just on the basis of chance. Perhaps this will add perspective to dramatic journalism and case portrayals that attribute an amazing degree of precision to the analyses of forensic investigation. For various reasons journalists, the general public, law enforcement and legal professionals, and sometimes forensic scientists themselves, are prone to representing forensic science as more exact than it really is. This volume simply cannot cover the entire field of forensic anthropology in all its diverse aspects. Its focus is not on practical laboratory or field procedures. Instead it examines the theoretical and methodological foundations of the discipline.

The cited bibliographic references are far from a comprehensive survey of the published literature relating to forensic anthropology. Many well-designed studies and instructive case reports have not been included, and non-inclusion should not be interpreted as an inference or innuendo of scientific shortcoming. This volume is intended to serve students in human skeletal biology as a basic, yet guided, tour of the research and practice of forensic anthropology at the dawn of the twenty-first century. Selection criteria for cited literature include historical importance and continuing influence, broadness of applicability in case work, promise of improved standards, level of methodological sophistication appropriate to the student or novice, or illustration of an important principle.

With the exception of a couple of material suppliers (FORDISC at University of Tennessee, Knoxville, and France Casting of Bellvue, Colorado), I have decided not to include lists of forensics-related websites, anatomical and anthropological equipment, laboratory suppliers, or commercial DNA laboratories, since all of these have a tendency to change with some regularity.

2

THE ROLE OF FORENSIC ANTHROPOLOGY IN HISTORICAL CONTEXT

THE SOMEWHAT DIFFICULT BIRTH OF A SPECIALTY

The application of skeletal biology to medical–legal investigations has its roots in nineteenth century legal medicine. Good overviews of this period can be found in Stewart (1979a) and Rhine (1998) and the references therein. The principal players at that time were Thomas Dwight, whom T. Dale Stewart dubbed the father of forensic anthropology, H. H. Wilder, and Jeffries Wyman and Oliver Wendell Holmes, both of whom testified at the "Harvard murder" trial of John Webster, who was convicted of murdering Harvard benefactor George Parkman. All four of these men pioneered what is today considered the field of forensic anthropology after being trained in anatomy or, in the case of Wilder, zoology.

From a more parochial viewpoint George A. Dorsey (1868–1931) could be considered the first full-fledged forensic anthropologist. In 1894 Dorsey was awarded the first Harvard Ph.D. in anthropology and only the second such degree in the country (Dorsey 1896). Although his career-long interests within anthropology were wide-ranging and later emphasized studies of Plains Indians and museology, it was his earlier efforts that impacted forensic anthropology. Dorsey's doctoral thesis on the mummies of a Peruvian necropolis was primarily archaeological. After a brief post-doctoral stint as an instructor at Harvard he

Fundamentals of Forensic Anthropology, by Linda L. Klepinger
Copyright © 2006 John Wiley & Sons, Inc.

moved to the Field Columbian Museum in Chicago, first as assistant curator of physical anthropology, and later as curator. He served there until 1915. During the final 10 years in Chicago he also held appointments as Professor of Comparative Anatomy at Northwestern University Dental School and Professor of Anthropology at the University of Chicago (Spencer, 1997; Ubelaker, 1999). It was during the final two decades of the nineteenth century that Dorsey published on human skeletal anatomy—including its medical–legal implications—although he must have been self-taught since he claimed in his dissertation to have had no formal training in osteology. Nevertheless, his expertise was summoned for the Luetgert murder trial, one of the most celebrated cases of the century (Giles and Klepinger, 1999). Loerzel (2003) provides a very thorough account of the Luetgert case, which is summarized here.

Adolph Luetgert, a 52-year-old German immigrant, had built his sausage factory on Chicago's near northwest side into the city's biggest. However, by early 1897 Luetgert's business was financially strapped, largely because of a swindle, and had to close down. By all accounts the financial tribulations were causing stress in the already troubled marriage of Adolph and his second wife, Louisa, sometimes rendered as the German spelling, Louise (Loerzel, 2003). Louisa Luetgert was undeniably last seen alive by her son on the night of 1 May 1897 at the Luetgert house on the sausage factory property. In response to subsequent inquiries by the children and Louisa's brother as to his wife's whereabouts, Adolph variously replied that she was off visiting or had run away. Six days later he reported Louisa missing to the police, who were suspicious and searched his factory. Of particular interest was a huge vat that held a thick, greasy, foul-smelling concoction that Luetgert explained was a boiled mixture of potash, fat, tallow and bone scraps used to make soft-soap to clean his factory. On the night of his wife's disappearance Luetgert had sent his watchman on two apparently needless errands and had been seen stirring the boiling vat. When the contents of the vat were strained, small pieces of bone appeared, and a search of the vat bottom produced two rings, one of which was a gold wedding band with the initials "L. L." on the inside. A sifted waste pile yielded more bone fragments and a corset stay.

The neighborhood rumor mill went into high gear, and the consumption of sausage dropped drastically in greater Chicagoland. A jump rope verse evolved (Baumann and O'Brien, 1986):

> Old man Luetgert made sausage out of his wife!
> He turned on the steam,
> His wife began to scream,
> There'll be a hot time in the old town tonight!

According to a former undergraduate student, the doggerel still survived in the neighborhood 90 years later. Never mind that sausage production had ceased some time before the fateful night in question.

From the beginning, Luetgert contended that his wife would eventually show up, and some reports of sighting of a woman fitting Louisa's description drifted in from various parts of the country. However, the police were persuaded of his guilt, and the vigorous investigation (which included placing an officer under the bed of the watchman, who feigned illness, in unfulfilled hopes of overhearing "smoking gun" evidence in the watchman's conversation with Luetgert) and equally vigorous prosecution furthered the careers of several of the principals.

Apparently "a speedy trial" had a more emphatic meaning in those days because Luetgert's first trial began in late August of the same year. Court records of the two trials have never been transcribed and are unavailable. However, contemporary newspaper and other accounts were quite detailed—often with direct quotations and question and answer format— offering the opportunity for fairly accurate reconstruction of important testimony. A primary challenge for the prosecution was demonstrating that Louisa Luetgert had, indeed, been murdered. The defense position was that the bone fragments represented bits of animals used in sausage manufacture and, therefore, should not be unexpected in the factory. There was also an issue of considerable laxity in the chain of custody of the bone fragments. Moreover, the location and circumstances of the discovery of several fragments were not totally clear.

At the first trial the *corpus delicti* was alleged to be represented by seven bones, all identified by Dorsey as being from a single individual—a human female. The direct and cross examination of several osteological experts representing both sides was contentious in the extreme, including what might best be characterized as a courtroom bone quiz. Of the osteological experts, the two who could be characterized as the "star witnesses" were Dorsey for the prosecution, and for the defense W. H. Allport, Professor of Anatomy at Northwestern University Medical School. Regarding the first trial cross examination of defense expert Allport, the *Chicago Times-Herald* (1 October 1897, p. 4) reported: "For the state he was handled by Mr. McEwen, and at his side sat Professor Dorsey, who felt that either his reputation as an osteologist or that of Allport must go by the board. Evidently Allport had the same idea in mind, and the battle was one that was rare and well worth seeing. In the conflict the fact that the life of a human being depended largely on the outcome was lost sight of, and from the minds of the combatants at least it faded from view. It was the reputation of Dorsey against that of Allport.

"To the lawyers, to the jurors, to the defendant, and to the average listener a great deal that was said was about as lucid as a jargon of Choctaw."

The acrimony between Dorsey and defense witnesses continued over the next few years and overflowed into regional scientific meetings (e.g. Ridlon, 1899). On 22 October the first trial ended in a hung jury with a vote of nine to three for conviction. The second trial began just five weeks later. Of the seven bones introduced at the first trial, the three largest, identified by Dorsey as a femoral shaft fragment, a petrous temporal, and a probable humeral head, were not in evidence in the second trial. Apparently the defense witnesses had cast sufficient doubt as to whether the femoral and humeral fragments were human at all, and the alleged temporal fragment had been essentially destroyed by falling into six or seven pieces and considerable dust as Dorsey and a Dr Pierce sawed the bone to aid in identification— before defense experts had a chance to identify it. This left only four pieces.

Dorsey identified the four pieces used in the second trial as a head of a rib, a head of a metacarpal, an entire sesamoid bone, and a phalanx of the fourth or fifth toe. It was said that all four of the pieces could be placed on a quarter without overlapping its edges (Christison, 1898; Fig. 2.1). Dorsey judged them to belong to one human body, that of a woman. It is interesting to note that, in the first trial, when Dorsey was shown all of the exhibits and was asked to go over them again and state which he was absolutely certain about, he answered that he was absolutely certain about the phalanx, the femur, the temporal, and the metacarpal (*Chicago Times-Herald*, 18 September 1897). Two of these four bones were not considered in the second trial. The totality of the osteological evidence of a *corpus delicti* introduced at the second trial can be seen in Figure 2.1. Nevertheless the jury found Luetgert guilty and opted for life imprisonment. Luetgert died in the Illinois State Penitentiary at Joliet on 27 July 1899, one hour before the delivery of a letter from his attorney assuring him that the money necessary for his appeal would at last be obtained in a few days.

Although osteological and dental testimony had been previously introduced in the courtroom, the Luetgert case placed Dorsey in the landmark position of the first *anthropologist* to testify in an American criminal trial. Much of the osteological testimony at the two trials was highly questionable, and Dorsey's contribution was no exception. Dorsey's testimony was controversial even at the time, and may explain, at least in part, why he never again ventured into the courtroom, nor did he publish in osteology after 1898. He resigned his museum and academic appointments in 1915 and, as they say, pursued other interests.

THE MIDDLE YEARS

A period of relative quiescence in forensic anthropology marked the early part of the twentieth century. Leading scholars, such as Ales Hrdlicka at

ALLEGED HUMAN BONE FRAGMENTS

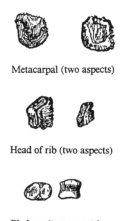

Metacarpal (two aspects)

Head of rib (two aspects)

Phalanx (two aspects)

Sesamoid (three aspects)

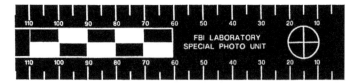

Figure 2.1   The four bone pieces used as evidence in the second Luetgert trial to scale with a quarter coin. Figure by Eugene Giles, modified from drawings in Christison (1898) that appear to be the only surviving depictions of the bones.

the Smithsonian Institution and Earnest Hooton at Harvard, consulted on legal cases, but forensic work was not central to their interests nor represented in their publications, aside from Hooton's one article in 1943. Until the outbreak of World War II the mantle for research on skeletal guides to human identification once again fell upon anatomists. Of these the most prominent American figure was T. Wingate Todd, professor of anatomy at Western Reserve University Medical School, who is most remembered for his contributions to the study of skeletal age markers.

Wilton Marion Krogman led the way for the twentieth century emergence of physical anthropology in forensic investigations. His article on the identification of human skeletal remains in the *FBI Law Enforcement Bulletin* (Krogman, 1939) brought the skills of osteologically trained physical anthropologists to the attention of law enforcement. To Krogman also goes the distinction of authoring the first textbook on the subject (Krogman, 1962).

World War II marked the first time that trained physical anthropologists, as well as anatomists, contributed to the recovery, identification, and repatriation of the remains of U.S. soldiers. A series of temporary identification units was established, with the central point for Europe located in Strasbourg and the central identification laboratory for the Pacific located in Hawaii. Wood and Stanley (1989) offer a summary of American anthropology's contribution to this effort. For the European Theater Harry Shapiro, Curator of Physical Anthropology at the American Museum of Natural History in New York, was called upon to offer recommendations on anthropological techniques for the identification of remains. The Europeans who actually carried out the identification procedures followed his recommendations. For the Pacific Theater Charles E. Snow, of the University of Kentucky was the first director of the Hawaii Central Identification Laboratory. In 1948 Mildred Trotter, an anatomist at Washington University in St Louis, succeeded Snow.

The recovery and identification operations that followed World War II and the Korean War presented an opportunity for research in the field of identification, albeit one that was, for all practical purposes, limited to sample populations of young men. Credit for the major persuasive push to do research goes to Mildred Trotter. Trotter's work on the estimation of stature from long bone length of a World War II sample is incorporated in the important standard (Trotter and Gleser, 1952) still in use to this day. Trotter's successful efforts greased the skids for research on the remains of American soldiers killed in action (KIA) and deceased prisoners of war (POW) from the Korean hostilities. T. Dale Stewart arranged for a leave of absence from the Smithsonian Institution to direct the collection of data on skeletal evidence of aging at the central identification unit in Kokura, Japan. In 1955 Thomas W. McKern went to Washington, DC to work with Stewart on the data collected by Stewart's identification team in Japan (which included Ellis R. Kerley and Charles P. Warren). The resulting report (McKern and Stewart, 1957) added substantially to our compendium of knowledge on skeletal indicators of age in young men. The various identification units established for World War II and Korean War casualties were temporary in their charter. The U.S. Army's mission on recovery and identification of the remains of U.S. service members continued in Thailand for the Indochina War. In 1976 the U.S. Army Central Identification Laboratory, Hawaii (CILHI) was established in Honolulu and continues in the recovery and identification of service members from past wars, as well as aiding in the identification of remains from recent disasters. In the fall of 2003 CILHI merged with the Joint Task Force-Full Accounting to form the Joint

POW/MIA Accounting Command (JPAC), still on Oahu. Its expanded personnel include several full-time anthropologists—on their web site they claim to employ 30 forensic anthropologists as of 2005. The wartime personal identification efforts stimulated the ongoing role of anthropologists in mass disasters, civilian as well as military.

The decade of the 1960s brought an expansion of interest in forensic anthropology. While a few physical anthropologists at the Smithsonian and at the Federal Aviation Administration participated in forensic investigations, a small, but influential, cohort of academic researchers devoted some research time and graduate curricular content to forensic objectives.

By 1971 Ellis Kerley opined that the number of anthropologists with a stake in forensics, through research or casework or both, had reached sufficient critical mass to establish their own section of the American Academy of Forensic Sciences (Snow, 1982). In 1972 the Physical Anthropology Section of the Academy was born. Since 1948 the Academy had been the umbrella organization for diverse professionals involved in the application of science to the law. In addition to Physical Anthropology, Academy Sections include Criminalistics, Engineering Sciences, General, Jurisprudence, Odontology, Pathology/Biology, Psychiatry and Behavioral Science, Questioned Documents, and Toxicology. Membership in the Physical Anthropology Section has grown from the original 14 to 267 in 2005. Kerley's leadership primed the 1977 establishment of the American Board of Forensic Anthropology, under the auspices of the Physical Anthropology Section of the Academy. The Board's mission is the examination and certification of anthropologists that it deems qualified to be designated Forensic Anthropologists. An initial cohort of established Ph.D. practitioners with supporting credentials was grandparented into certification; after 1978 formal examination was added to the requirements.

The 1980s ushered in a new dimension to forensic anthropology: investigation of human rights abuses. In 1983 a brutal and repressive military dictatorship that had begun in 1976 in Argentina ended. During the tenure of the military regime, thousands of Argentineans had been "disappeared." In 1984 Clyde Snow traveled to Argentina as a consultant in the recovery and identification of cadavers of presumptive "disappeared" persons that were being exhumed from unmarked graves in various local cemeteries (Joyce and Stover, 1991). Snow quickly realized that little usable forensic evidence would be recovered from the heavy-handed grave openings. Under Snow's leadership a small group of students was trained in scientific exhumation and skeletal identification and analysis. In 1984 the Argentine Forensic Anthropology Team, or Equipo Argentino de Anthropología Forense (EAAF), was founded, not only in response to the need to exhume and identify "disappeared" persons, but also to investigate and document human rights abuses. The EAAF's mission soon extended beyond the boundaries of Argentina, and it is now one of global investigations of atrocities. Other international organizations have joined the effort to document human rights abuses and identify the victims (Burns, 1998). Forensic anthropologists have been major contributors to these missions, whose work is typically exhausting, often disheartening, and frequently dangerous. Those interested in participating in such endeavors should read Steadman and Haglund's (2005) overview of the work of anthropologists in human rights investigations.

In the final decade of the twentieth century forensic anthropologists were recruited to participate in a formal national system for the identification and mortuary disposition of victims of mass disasters. Ten regional Disaster Mortuary Operational Response Teams (DMORTs) were organized under the National Disaster Medical System (NDMS). The DMORT teams utilize the services of forensic anthropologists along with pathologists, funeral directors, forensic odontologists, fingerprint specialists, X-ray technicians, and other specialists in establishing temporary morgue facilities, victim identification, processing, preparation, and disposition of human remains. Beginning in 1993, one or more of the regional DMORT teams has been deployed on declared national disasters that have involved cemetery floods, hurricane, a series of airplane crashes, and the bombing of the Alfred P. Murrah Federal Building in Oklahoma City. All 10 regional teams were simultaneously activated for the first time following the destruction of the New York World Trade Center on 11 September 2001.

APPROACHING SENESCENCE?

The need for skill in forensic anthropology has expanded in recent decades. What began as largely a quest for personal identification from skeletonized remains now frequently encompasses assessments of decomposed, burned, and fully fleshed remains—even occasionally the living. Requested analyses frequently center on evidence of time since death, circumstances of body disposition, perimortem trauma, dismemberment, past abuse or neglect, and evidence recovery.

The demand for competent forensic analyses is not likely to abate in the near future. As with odontology, anthropology has not been completely superceded by the technology of DNA analysis. Even when recoverable from remains, DNA analysis is constrained by the need for appropriate comparisons to arrive at a positive identification. Biological profiling narrows an initially vast universe of candidates to a shorter, hopefully more manageable, short list. DNA addresses only the question of identification; it sheds no light on the other forensic questions that may be amenable to anthropological techniques.

All of this is not to say that the practice of forensic anthropology does not face significant challenges. Foremost among these is implementing quality control. There are no licenses. In many jurisdictions those charged with death investigations are naive to the field and cannot distinguish the competently and appropriately trained from the wannabe. During budget crunches, expenses of anthropological analyses fall to the bottom of the pecking order. However, educational efforts and successful track records can ameliorate these sorts of hurdles.

A more nagging problem, at least for the near future, lies in the training of forensic anthropologists for casework. The most basic skill is an intimate, hands-on familiarity with skeletal material representing all ages and including fragmentary disarticulated and isolated elements. The curricular track for those entering forensic anthropology has traditionally been a laboratory course in human osteology followed by extensive work in bioarchaeology. However, in North America institutional resources have been shrinking, and despite continuing high student interest, current prevalent academic philosophy and political considerations frequently discourage the continuation of programs and training in areas of forensic and bioarchaeological bent. Opportunities for the sort of practical training enjoyed by the current gray eminences are contracting. The level of expertise sought by those requesting consultation in forensic anthropology cannot be achieved solely by turning to textbooks, websites, or skeletal casts. It appears that there is already a disconnect between the increasing demand for forensic anthropology services and the number of people able to provide them. The dilemma is not unsolvable; the situation will require both the political will of institutions and the hustle of young investigators to acquire replacements for disappearing skeletal collections. Unfortunately, the latter task is not one generally rewarded at tenure and promotion review. Neither is applied anthropology.

PART II

TOWARDS PERSONAL IDENTIFICATION

3

INITIAL ASSESSMENTS OF SKELETAL REMAINS

As with their journalistic counterparts, four questions summarize the typical investigative goals of forensic anthropology: What? Who? When? How? The answers to what (or, is it human?) and when (or, is it recent enough to be of forensic interest?) may quickly direct what, if any, further inquiry should be made. If remains are contemporary and human, the next task is usually to attach a name to the skeleton, often approached by comparing skeletal demographic data assessments with missing persons reports.

A variety of factors impede getting an accurate handle on the scope of the problem. The first is that statistics on the numbers of missing persons, children and adults, are not currently part of the FBI's Uniform Crime Report. However, some other sources give a broad approximation. According to the Nation's Missing Children Organization and Center for Missing Adults (NMCO), as of March 2003 there were 97,297 active missing persons cases in the United States, of which a little over 54,000 were juveniles, and a little over 43,000 were aged 18 and older. In this case the figure can be confusing or misleading, especially for juveniles. The Department of Justice estimates that 800,000 children are reported missing each year, but most are taken by a noncustodial parent; others run away or are abandoned. Estimates for 1999 found that 115 children were abducted by a stranger that year. Considerations of the latter statistics appear to be reflected in the former figures. The missing children abducted by strangers and runaways are at

Fundamentals of Forensic Anthropology, by Linda L. Klepinger
Copyright © 2006 John Wiley & Sons, Inc.

highest probability for matching recovered remains. However, children, and adults for that matter, dying as the result of intentional or unintentional acts of family members or acquaintances may never be reported as missing.

Analyses of skeletonized or macerated remains can involve discriminations that would be much more straightforward on fresh or well-preserved specimens. The challenge of the task rises with the incompleteness and friability of the material. The first agendum is determining, for each skeletal element, whether it is human or non-human. If the remains are human then the number of individuals represented needs to be determined or approximated. When multiple individuals, including human–nonhuman mixtures, are present, then meaningful versus spurious associations are useful distinctions, albeit frequently not obtainable with certainty.

HUMAN OR NOT?

Probably about 20 percent or more of questions addressed to the physical anthropologist involve discrimination of human from nonhuman remains. This was the primary charge to anthropologists working at the Staten Island Fresh Kills Landfill after the destruction of the World Trade Center. As puzzling as this charge first sounded to some of us who had not been familiar with the World Trade Center, it quickly became obvious that the many restaurants that had been within the complex of buildings had made a substantial contribution of skeletal parts.

In most cases the most appropriate and straightforward criterion for distinguishing human skeletal parts from those of nonhuman animals is morphology. If the analyst is intimately familiar with human bones and teeth, especially when the material is broken and incomplete, then he usually can recognize an element, or piece of an element, that lies outside the range of human morphology. Mastery of adult skeletal material is not enough; immature human bones pose serious identification pitfalls for the unwary. Infant and child bone may bear little resemblance to the adult counterpart, and by that token be attributed to a small animal. An infant maxilla, although a single bone, looks very different from the more mature version. It is doubtful whether anybody knowing only the adult skeleton would recognize many of the unfused portions of sacral and pre-sacral vertebrae, especially if recovered in isolation. Conversely, very small single-piece vertebrae or sacra cannot be human, no matter how much the morphology may (superficially) resemble the human. It is a good idea to remember the approximate size of these human elements when they are first united into a single bone.

A raccoon baculum (penis bone) can somewhat resemble a young child's clavicle. Making morphological distinctions between human and other animal bone does not require training in faunal identification, although further species identification may gratify curiosity.

In situations of high breakage or poor preservation, morphological traits may be ambiguous or missing altogether. Other traits of vertebrate bone can be useful in the sorting out. Bird bone is lightly built with thin-cortex tubular long bones, which might resemble human metacarpals, metatarsals, and infant long bones. However, the pneumatic bird bone sometimes has internal bony struts (Young, 1981). Turtle or tortoise carapace (dorsal shell) and plastron (ventral shell) have plates with some sutural borders and can resemble thin infant or child cranial bone. In young animals where sutures have not fused, the plates separate on decomposition just as an infant skull does. Since turtle shell is bone (Romer, 1949), simple scanning of chemical spectra will not distinguish it from human bone, but careful morphological observation will.

Distinctions between human and other mammalian bone can be more difficult when the bone is fragmentary and the more diagnostic portions of the elements, e.g. ends of long bones as opposed to the shafts, are missing. Ungulate bone is noticeably more dense than human and preserves quite well. The hardness of ungulate bone makes it harder to scratch and produces a different tonal quality when tapped with a fingernail or similar instrument. For those who have access to the necessary equipment, such as a heavy-duty microtome, thin sections of ungulate cortical bone appear different from human bone sections under the microscope: patterns of osteons may appear qualitatively distinct from human ones, and subperiosteal lamellar ungulate bone has a folded-over (plexiform) appearance not found in human bone.

The posterior teeth of humans differ substantially from other animals in North America, as do the anterior teeth in many cases. Some teeth and tooth fragments can be problematical. Such cases usually can be keyed out with reference figures or collections. Very small fragments, however, can be impossible to assign on morphological criteria.

One cannot leave the topic of human–animal distinctions without mention of the now-traditional bear paw deception. Figure 3.1 is a radiograph of a skinned and desiccated bear forepaw found in rural east central Illinois. The intact specimen bore a devilishly close resemblance to a human hand. The hindpaw of a bear can mimic the human foot (Stewart, 1979a; Hoffman, 1984) to a similar extent. Granted, the presence of claws on a bear paw would quickly give away its identity, but these are typically missing because the distal phalanges are cut off when the hide is removed. The very nature of the phalangeal cuts should raise suspicions about a possible bear. Also suspicious on the radiograph are the paired radio-opaque areas about the distal metacarpals, which result from multiple sesamoid bones in far greater numbers than are ever found in humans. One might reasonably consider that in most areas of the country the chances of being asked to identify

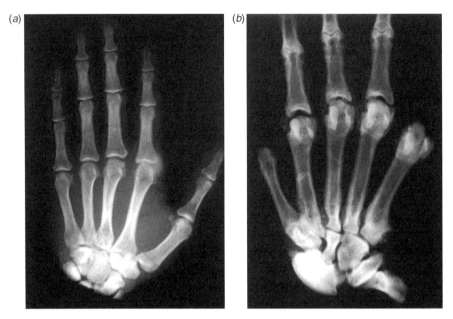

Figure 3.1   Radiographs of human hand, left, and bear forepaw, right.

a bear paw are vanishingly small, but not so. Probably because butchery often takes place some distance from the kill site, bear paws show up where there are no bears—east central Illinois is a case in point.

Finally, some inorganic materials can appear deceptively human. Some building insulating materials can bear a striking resemblance to human hair, and small, plain, unglazed potsherds can look like cranial bones at first glance. If you are in the field, in a hurry and in doubt, bag it and sort it out later in the laboratory.

NUMBER OF INDIVIDUALS REPRESENTED

The first task as analysis begins is to lay out all of the skeletal elements in anatomical order and take an inventory. Duplicated elements quickly become obvious. Two left ulnae indicate two individuals, but 13 thoracic vertebrae may not—especially if there are no other indications of multiple individuals. Commingling of remains of multiple individuals may also be detected by noting any elements that are incompatible with others on the basis of age, sex, size, robusticity, or configuration. People are bilaterally symmetrical, although often not completely or minutely so. There may be impossible joint articulations that signal that more than one person is present. Compatibility of the atlanto-occipital joint condyles can be particularly helpful in establishing cranium–postcranium unity. Normal morphology of the condyles varies considerably; for instance, there may be single or dual facets and different degrees of curvature from one individual to another. However, the size and shape of the occipital condyles always mirror the size and shape of the corresponding atlas condyles. This articular match can be valuable when a cranium rolls or is carried a considerable distance from the rest of the body. The temporal-mandibular articulation is another frequently useful key to establishing whether one or two individuals are represented. Ubelaker (2002) has reviewed the leading methods for tackling the problem of commingled remains.

Most forensic anthropologists and bioarchaeologists are familiar with the minimum number of individuals (MNI) formulation in which the most commonly occurring element, for example, the left femur, is counted. There are a few judgment calls, such as whether two different portions of an element, say a proximal and distal end, come from one body or two. In such a situation judgment is made on the basis of compatibility with regard to attributes such as size or maturity and whether there is any degree of anatomical feature overlap between the two fragments. Nevertheless, the method is extremely simple and frequently adequate to the task at hand. It yields, however, a very conservative number, and in the case of mass disasters and especially in the case of large mass graves, it is most likely an overly conservative number because sets of individual remains not containing the single most commonly iterated element will not be counted. Since the theoretical maximum number of individuals can equal the number of elements, it is a less informative number than MNI.

West and Giles (2001) have called attention to ways of estimating the original number of individuals in the killed population, known as the probable number of individuals (PNI). The Lincoln Index approach (Lincoln, 1930) originated from wildlife recapture studies in which live captured animals are marked and released to the wild population. The proportion of marked animals that are subsequently recaptured is assumed to be equal to the proportion of marked animals in the total wild population. By analogy, elements from one side can be equivalent to the number of marked and released animals, and elements from the opposite side equivalent to the number of individuals trapped in the second sampling; the number of paired elements corresponds to the recaptured individuals. Thus, the counts of the right and left sides of an element are multiplied and then divided by he number of matched pairs (P) of that element:

$$\text{PNI} = (R \times L)/P$$

With small samples and small numbers of pairs there is a better, unbiased formula that has the added advantage of avoiding infinitely high estimates when there are no matched pairs (Seber, 1982):

$$PNI = (L + 1)(R + 1)/(P + 1) - 1$$

If there are no right–left pairs, the formula conveniently reduces to

$$PNI = (R + 1)(L + 1)$$

Confidence intervals can be calculated (Seber, 1982).

Another formulation is derived from archaeological estimates of faunal abundances (Krantz, 1968). The estimated number of individuals is still derived from the counts of left, right, and paired elements:

$$N = (L^2 + R^2)/2P$$

This estimate is less conservative than the Lincoln Index formulations because it allow greater contribution of unmatched elements to the assemblage estimate. If right and left side counts are equal, the Lincoln and Krantz methods produce the same PNI, and if all elements are paired (as with complete skeletons), PNI = MNI. The advantage of PNI estimates over MNI estimates is that PNI formulations partially account for unrecovered bodies or portions of bodies in the victim count; MNI addresses solely the recovered remains. The PNI estimates' potential for taking unexcavated portions of graves or sites into account becomes increasingly valuable as the number of mass graves and death sites overwhelms the ability to thoroughly excavate and analyze the victims' remains in a timely fashion.

The ultimate commingling nightmare is usually any inquiry involving cremains (cremated remains). The scale may vary from the contents of a single funerary urn to multiple cartons, and the degree of fragmentation can also vary over a considerable range. For containers supposedly carrying the cremains of a single individual, the question is usually whether any remains of another individual are included and usually arises from suspected fraudulent or negligent funerary care. Improper disposal of cremains can sometime result in massive accumulations, and in such cases MNI estimates are all that are practical, even though such numbers may grossly underestimate the true representation in the death assemblage.

4

ASSIGNMENT OF SEX

CRITERIA FOR SEX ATTRIBUTION IN THE ADULT SKELETON

On my first bioarchaeological field task outside of North America I began my evaluation on the first burials uncovered. The first dozen or so were partial and lacked pelves, so I proceeded to assign sex primarily on the basis of skull characteristics as I had learned them from experience with the predominant historic and prehistoric North American groups—rookie mistake. Almost all appeared and measured more feminine than masculine, an impression dispelled by the arrival of burials complete with pelvic remains. I had failed to appreciate that the skulls of some populations are considerably more robust than the skulls of other populations, and the North American groups tended toward robusticity. Larger skeletal size and greater muscularity characterize the males *vis-à-vis* females of the same population. *Within* a population is the operative condition; there are no precise size and robusticity standards that are universally applicable. Moreover, population differences in the degree of skeletal sexual dimorphism need to be taken into account, as do sexual dimorphism differences in adult height in different ethnic groups (Eveleth, 1975). The point of this tale is that metric and nonmetric standards are meant to be applied to the groups

Fundamentals of Forensic Anthropology, by Linda L. Klepinger
Copyright © 2006 John Wiley & Sons, Inc.

from which they were derived or for which they have demonstrated suitability. Pelvic morphological features are an exception to that rule.

Sexual dimorphism in the skeleton reflects a history of differential selective pressures that are mediated primarily by adolescent hormonal output. The following discussion concentrates on those traits that, for most observers, are the ones most easily evaluated when applied to a single individual. The systematic bias of my skull evaluations in favor of females reflects the fact that I was dealing with a more cranially gracile population than I was accustomed to. In fact, the opposite bias in sexing skeletal material is more often the case (Weiss, 1972).

Pelvic Traits

The distinctive human pelvis shape as an adaptation to posture and locomotion is shared by both sexes. The added selective pressure of carrying and giving birth to large-brained babies is borne only by the female. Thus, it is no surprise that the pelvic area exhibits the greatest sexual dimorphism and can be regarded as the "gold standard" for sexual discrimination. A very long inventory of innominate (os coxae, pelvic bone) traits has been demonstrated to have significant differences in all populations of males and females.

Elongating the pubic body and ramus in the lateral-medial direction is a very efficient way to increase the roominess of the female pelvic basin. This pubic stretch produces the inverted U-shaped subpubic angle in females that contrasts with the inverted V-shaped angle in males (Figs 4.1c and d and 4.2). It is also a major contributor, along with shorter female ischium length, to the greater pubis/ischium ratio in females (Washburn, 1948).

Phenice (1969) tested three visual pubic traits for sex determination: the presence of the ventral arc, subpubic concavity (i.e. U-shaped), and narrow, ridged medial aspect of the ischio-pubic ramus in the female, contra no ventral arc, broad medial aspect of the ischial-pubic ramus, and no recurved subpubic angle in males (Fig. 4.1). On a sample of 275 pubes he found the suite of three traits to be 96 percent correct in assigning sex. Others had less success (e.g. Lovell, 1989). Sutherland and Suchey (1991) then tried the technique on a large ($n = 1284$) documented sample of pubes from the Office of the Chief Medical Examiner–Coroner of Los Angeles. The ventral arc alone provided 96 percent accuracy. The lateral subpubic recurve could not be tested on this sample, and the criterion of presence or absence of the ridge on the ischio-pubic ramus produced a disappointing 70 percent accuracy. (I also find this trait either hard to evaluate or unreliable.) Sutherland and Suchey also point out that a precursor ventral arc appears on girls in their teens and becomes better defined in the 20s. In

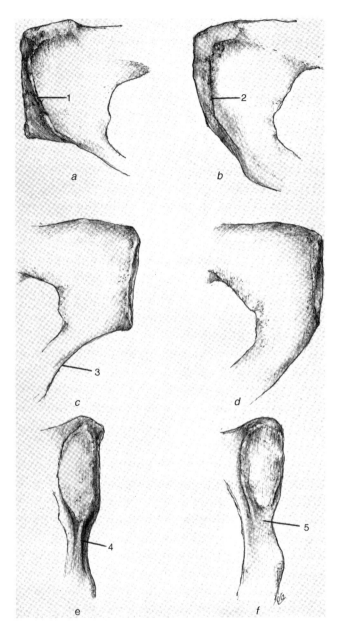

Figure 4.1   (*a*-1) Ventral arc on ventral surface of the female pubis. (*b*-2) Slight ridge on ventral aspect of male pubis. (*c*-3) Subpubic concavity seen from dorsal aspect of female pubis and ischio-pubic ramus. (*d*) Dorsal aspect of male pubis and ischio-pubic ramus. (*e*-4) Ridge on medial aspect of female ischio-pubic ramus. (*f*-5) Broad medial surface of male ischio-pubic ramus. Reprinted from Phenice, T. W. (1969) *American Journal of Physical Anthropology* by permission of John Wiley & Sons.

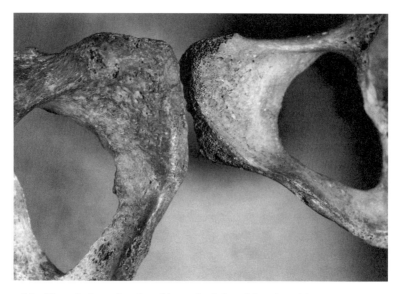

Figure 4.2   Ventral view of male pubis on the left and female pubis on the right. Note the difference in subpubic angles and the presence of a ventral arc on the female.

males a ventral line may parallel the symphyseal edge, but Sutherland and Suchey caution that, in about four percent of male pubes, it could be confused with the ventral arc. Ubelaker and Volk's (2002) test of the Phenice method on 198 Terry collection skeletons suggested that experience was a factor in obtaining a high degree of accuracy and that using additional pelvic morphology indicators enhanced accuracy, especially for the less experienced. It is interesting to note that the two consistently misclassified male pelves exhibited ventral lines that closely resembled ventral arcs.

Of the pelvic traits listed in Table 4.1, not all are of equal value. The pubic traits have great diagnostic value, but the pubis is not the sturdiest skeletal element and can be badly damaged by harsh postmortem conditions. The sciatic notch and sacro-iliac articular areas of the ilium are more resilient to damage and possess good diagnostic value (Fig. 4.3).

The visual assessment of pelvic traits is reliable enough to render metric methods unnecessary. Although more amenable to statistical analyses, metric methods have the drawback of landmarks that are often hard to define and higher interobserver error (see discussion by Adams and Byrd, 2002).

The Skull

Although the skull is not the next best skeletal region for assessing sex—that standing probably belongs to the femur or humerus—it is commonly

TABLE 4.1   Pelvic Traits Characteristic of Sex

Trait	Male	Female
Pubic symphysis	Broad, more triangular, more biconvex anterior–posteriorly	More narrow and rectangular; flat posteriorly and convex anteriorly
Greater sciatic notch	Deep, more acute angle	Wide and shallow
Ilia	High, more upright	Lower, more flaring in upper part
Acetabula	Larger, more forwardly directed	Smaller, more laterally directed
Preauricular sulcus	Generally absent to small	Commonly better developed
Iliac auricular surfaces	Not elevated from surrounding bone	Partially or completely elevated
Ischio-pubic ramus	Broader, less everted	Often everted with ridge
Ventral arc	Absent	Present
Subpubic arch	V-shaped	Broader U-shaped
Dorsal pubic pits	Absent	Sometimes present
Obturator foramina	Larger, more oval	Smaller, more triangular
Sacrum	Relatively high and narrow	Shorter and broader, less curved in upper portion
Pelvic inlet	Heart-shaped	More elliptic, more spacious
True pelvis	Smaller	Shallow, more spacious, less encroached by ischial spines

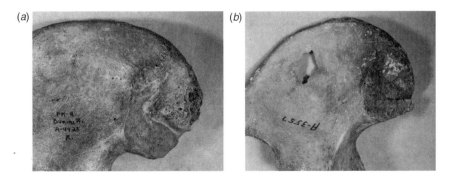

Figure 4.3   (*a*) On the left a male ilium with nonelevated auricular surface, minimal preauricular sulcus, and narrow greater sciatic notch. (*b*) On the right a female ilium with elevated auricular surface, large preauricular sulcus, and wide greater sciatic notch.

encountered in isolation or with elements of even less diagnostic value. Population differences in skull dimorphism can be considerable, and frequently population traits and sex traits may be confounded. Variability in the degree of sexual dimorphism within and between populations probably reflects some combination of genetic and environmental factors, and life histories. Consequently, even within a population, the degree of sexual dimorphism can fluctuate on both short and long time scales. The degree of fluctuation is usually not a matter of concern, but it is a small factor that can negatively sway previous estimates of accuracy if conditions have significantly changed. Ignoring such contingencies, with comparable preservation of the skull and other elements, the degree of sex assignment certainty drops considerably from the pelvic standards.

Visual Assessment   Many forensic situations do not allow for a preliminary assessment of the range of variation within a group, but present only one or a few skulls for diagnosis. The traits listed in Table 4.2 are those most commonly used in discriminating the sexes, but not all are of equal reliability. For instance, the external occipital protuberance ranges from no salient relief to a well-developed downward projecting spur or plate, sometimes referred to as an inion hook. While projecting occipital protuberances are more typical of male skulls, they can also appear on females, and are sometimes quite large. Conversely, male protuberances can be quite modest (see Gülekon and Turgut, 2003 for a discussion). Other cranial traits can also

TABLE 4.2   Skull Traits Characteristic of Sex

Trait	Male	Female
Size of vault, face, teeth	Larger	Smaller
Robustness	Greater muscularity relief	Less relief
Supraorbital ridges	More pronounced	Less pronounced
Superior border of orbit	Dull	Sharp
Forehead	More retreating	Rounded, frontal eminences frequent
Mastoid process	Longer, more robust	Shorter, less robust
Occipital muscle attachments	Nuchal crests	Nuchal lines or ridges
External occipital protuberance	Well developed	Occasionally well developed
Posterior zygomatic arch	Extends past auditory meatus as a ridge	Less stout, generally ends at auditory meatus
Chin	Squared off	Rounded
Gonial angle	Close to right angle	More obtuse angle
Gonial region	Flaring	Little flare
Ascending ramus	Stouter, broader	Narrower with smaller coronoid process

display a wide range of within-sex variation. The final sex classification reflects the direction of a majority of the traits. Some skulls have most of the traits pointing strongly in the direction of one sex. One is more confident about the sex assignment of such skulls. However, many skulls are more ambiguous in both degree and count of sexually diagnostic traits; these engender less confident assignment or no assignment at all (indeterminant). An additional factor needs to be considered. With increasing age, the morphology of the cranium appears progressively more masculine (Meindl *et al.*, 1985a; Walker, 1995). The trend toward accentuation of male characteristics holds for both males and females, so a preliminary rough evaluation for age is advisable to take that into account.

The degree of confidence in sex assignment from visual evaluation is hard to quantify. In their textbooks on forensic osteology Krogman (1962) and Stewart (1979a) report their results on trials of skulls alone from the Todd and Terry collections, respectively. Stewart reported 77 percent accuracy, and Krogman estimated that his success at large (not in a collection he knew to be about 93 percent male) would be 82–87 percent. These were men with a tremendous amount of experience in analyzing skeletons; presumably beginners would do much worse.

Discriminant Function Analysis   In response to mediocre success of "eyeballing" crania and next to no control over error rate estimation, R. A. Fisher's statistical tool for classification was enlisted into the service of forensics. For any measurable trait the ranges of values for males and females overlap to a greater or lesser extent. The smaller the area of overlap, the more often sex can be assigned with reasonable surety. Multivariate discriminant function analysis minimizes overlap for several traits at a time. It does this by seeking a linear combination of weighted variables (variables = measurements) that maximizes the between-groups variance relative to the within-groups variance. Essentially this is maximizing an *F* ratio. The weights for the measurements (variables) are derived from a database of measurements taken on a series of individuals of known sex, and the weights are themselves measures of the discriminatory potential of the measurement (at least for that series). In other words, the method offers a straightforward statistical basis for deciding, on the basis of multiple measurements, whether an individual is more likely to be a member of one or another of two well-defined groups—male or female.

The discriminant function takes the form of an equation:

$$Y = w_1X_1 + w_2X_2 + \cdots + w_nX_n$$

where w = weight, X = variable, and n = number of variables.

The sectioning point is that value of Y that maximizes the between-groups to within-groups ratio more than any other linear combination of weighted Xs. The Y-value for any given unknown skull is then compared with the sectioning point Y-value to decide its male or female assignment. In most cases, although not always, the numbers higher than the sectioning point (which is often zero) are male, and those lower are female.

The 1963 Giles and Elliot paper on sex determination by multivariate functional analysis of crania got the ball rolling for forensic anthropology. Their discriminant functions were based on measurements of 300 crania from the Terry and Hamann–Todd collections that were divided equally into the four groups of white and black males and females, with 108 held out for a test sample. The sample ages ranged from 21 to 75 years. The 21 discriminant functions differed on the basis of the number and selection of utilized measurements and the racial classification(s) of the database for that sample. The calculated probability of misclassification is listed for each of the functions, so one picks the function with the lowest chance of misclassification that is compatible with the measurements obtainable and presumed ethnicity of the cranium in question. The 95 percent level listed for each function refers to the 95 percent confidence level for the reference sample on which the function was based. It reflects the confidence level for the general population only insofar as the reference sample is a random sample of the general population. In other words, the confidence levels are a best case estimate—casework levels of confidence at those scores will be lower.

Because sex discriminate functions are so dependent on size, these formulae can be effectively used only on those populations whose cranial size approximates that of the database. For such populations as the North American Amerindians, the success rate seems comparable to that of white and black Americans. Correct sex classifications are in the range of high 70s to 90 percent for test cases—about the same as visual evaluation by experienced workers. Calcagno (1981) has pointed out that the size differences among populations mean that a discriminant function that is very successful for one population may misclassify many in another population. He also warned that attempting to compensate for size variations among populations by adjusting the sectioning point is not a solution.

For the inexperienced observer discriminant function analysis provides a more solid foundation for attribution of sex from the cranium and takes the subjective guesswork out of "eyeballing" decisions. However, there are limitations. The accuracy of specific equations falls if they are applied to individuals who differ, especially in size, from those constituting the original database. The broader the ethnic representation within the database, the broader the applicability of the function—albeit often at the expense of some accuracy. One should match the function to the specific case as closely as possible, but when in doubt, a broader database is better. The technique cannot be relied upon to resolve tough "borderline" decisions. All too often, what appears to be borderline morphologically produces a discriminant function value close to the sectioning point. These same considerations apply to Giles' (1964) mandibular discriminant functions. Those workers using PC systems will wish to investigate the latest (3.0) FORDISC program available from the University of Tennessee, Knoxville. Again, the same considerations and precautions discussed above apply to these (or any) discriminant functions.

All of the Giles and Elliot functions relied on some portion of the cranial vault and/or face. For those occasions when a fragmentary cranium is represented solely by the basilar portions, Holland (1986) has devised equations from a sample of 100 blacks and whites from the Terry collection. On a holdout sample of 20 skulls, the various equations using measurements from the condylar/foramen magnum area of the occipital were accurate 70–85 percent of the time. The number of variables needed for the six equations went from two to nine. I know of no attempts at visual morphological assessment of that region, but I would bet that any such efforts would yield notably poorer results.

The Appendicular Bones

Femur   Next to the pelvis and skull the sexual dimorphism of the femur has received the most attention, probably because the femur is likely to be recovered. The mean length of the femur, or of any long bone for that matter, is larger for males than for females, reflecting mean stature differences. However, the length by itself is not really an effective discriminator any more than stature is. The angle of the neck of the femur to the shaft is smaller in females, but the trait is difficult to assess accurately and reproducibly.

Basing their work on 98 male and 101 female African Americans from the Terry Collection, Thieme and Schull (1957) found that the diameter of the head was the best single femoral discriminator. The discriminating value of 44 mm, half the difference between the mean value for each sex, best separated the males and females of their sample. They do not describe how the measurement was taken. Interestingly, Stewart (1979a) reported measuring the maximum head diameter of a racially mixed sample of 50 males and 50 females from the same collection and getting a smaller range of values and a noticeably smaller overlap that centered about 45 mm. Stewart's sample was half the size, and the measurement only presumably the same, so any attribution of cause for the discrepancy is a conjecture. France (1998), in her review of attribution of sex from the skeleton, presented data from various sources on femoral head diameter from African Americans, European Americans, and archaeological Native Americans. The female averages ranged from 41.9 to 42.4, and the males from 49.0 to 47.0. The listed cutoff points were all ± 1 mm or less of 45 mm, and percentage accuracies for the samples ranged from mid 80s to low 90s. A cutoff point of 45.5 would best fit the modern American data; the archaeological skeletons were a little smaller.

A recent application of discriminant functions for assessing sex from the femur (Šlaus et al., 2003) reaffirms the valuable degree of sexual dimorphism displayed by this bone. For seven discriminant functions (two of them based on single measurements) applied to 195 Croatian war dead, they report accuracies from 96.7 to 89.0 percent on reclassifying the test sample. The accuracy figures, however, represent a best case scenario: the reclassification of the test sample. Figures for the functions applied to other population samples are bound to be lower. It is interesting to note that the single measurement of maximum diameter of the head was competitive with functions utilizing more measurements, and that if the male–female demarcation was the mean of the average for each sex, that demarcation point was 45.45 mm.

Maximum diameter of the head has been consistently voted the single best femoral trait for assigning sex. For most modern European-derived and African-derived populations living in developed countries the sectioning point of 45.5 mm will probably predict sex at least as well as the skull; that is, accurate about 80 percent of the time is a conservative estimate. If you know the ethnicity and have functions based on that population, you can do better.

In the event of skeletal fragmentation when the femoral head is missing or damaged, femoral circumference at midshaft is a fallback (Black, 1978). DiBennardo and Taylor (1979) found that, about 83 percent of the time, a circumference equal to or greater than 86 mm indicated male, and a circumference of 85 mm or less indicated female on reference and test samples totaling 115 from a white dissecting room collection. Accuracy on the ethnically diverse general population is unknown, but likely to be 80 percent or less. When applied to geographically or ethnically different groups, any such metric discriminator is apt to perform much worse. For instance, Frutos (2003) reported that value of the minimum superior-inferior femoral neck diameter based on North American material performed abysmally as a sex criterion on a rural Guatemalan population.

Humerus Perforation of the olecranon-coronoid septum of the distal humerus is found significantly more often in females than in males and is related to differences in humerus robusticity (Benfer and McKern, 1966). Dwight (1905) and Stewart (1979a) both tended to favor the head of the humerus as being more reliably dimorphic than the head of the femur. For the vertical head diameter Stewart, using 50 males and 50 females from the Terry collection, revised Dwight's figures based on 400 anatomical specimens to adjust for absence of articular cartilage. His dividing line was 45 mm with 45 to 43 mm being probably female, less than 43 very likely female, and 45 to 47 mm probably male and above 47 mm almost certainly male. For a larger sample from the Terry Collection France (1998) lists 44.7 and 45 mm vertical diameter as cutoffs for blacks and whites, respectively; she also lists transverse diameter cutoffs of 42.2 mm for both groups. These numbers correctly classified her sample about 90 percent of the time.

Rogers (1999) reported a similar degree of accuracy for four visual traits of the distal humerus: trochlear constriction, trochlear symmetry, olecranon fossa shape and depth, and angle of the medial epicondyle. The method, developed on whites from the Toronto Grant Collection, was tested on whites from the W. M. Bass Donated Skeletal Collection at the University of Tennessee ($n = 93$) and from the University of New Mexico Collection ($n = 35$). These results are promising, but leave the system untested on non-white groups, and interobserver error might be significant. Therefore, workers should follow the trait evaluation procedures in the original article carefully. Because the distal humerus is more often recovered intact and unscathed than the head, this method offers a valuable option for fragmentary material, and extension to more extensive testing and racially diverse material would contribute to its usefulness.

Other Appendicular Elements   İşcan and Miller-Shaivitz (1984a, b) and Holland (1991) have investigated dimorphic aspects of the tibia in samples of blacks and whites from the Terry ($n = 159$) and Hamann–Todd ($n = 100$) Collections respectively. France (1998) also looked at 135 black and white tibiae from the Tennessee Data Bank. In general, when the proximal epiphysis measures were included in the regressions or discriminant functions, they did better than other tibial dimensions. Scores from the reference samples (for functions based on various proximal epiphyseal measures) ranged from 86 to 95 percent correct assignment. However, Bass (1995) noted that studies from other parts of the world reinforced the earlier works' indication that the metric-based functions are highly population-specific. If the ethnic/racial affiliation is unknown, it would be advisable to go with other standards that are less population-sensitive than the tibia, if possible.

Berrizbeitia's (1989) study of the maximal and minimal diameters of the radial head suggested that, at least for measurements more than a couple of millimeters away from the sectioning points, acceptable sex decisions could be made. However, the exact meaning of the accuracy figures is not clear. France (1998) has estimates from functions derived from the Tennessee Data Bank for radius and ulna. So far rigorous tests of the accuracy and limitations of the forearm bones for assessing sex have not been published.

In the early 1990s Scheur and Elkington (1993) derived regression equations for six measurements taken on the five metacarpals and the first proximal phalanx. Their reference sample was 60 white British individuals, and the equations were tested on a holdout sample of 20. The five best equations were based on metacarpals 1–3 and the first proximal phalanx, and yielded accuracy ranges from 74 to 94 percent on the small test sample, with metacarpal one topping the list. From a sample of 40 of each black and white males and females, Smith (1996) produced discriminant functions for all the right and left metacarpals and phalanges. Models for sex classification gave a mathematically estimated range of 88.7–94.4 percent correctly classified. A serious impediment to this method is the difficult to impossible assignment of phalanges 2–5 to side and ray. Two equations use metacarpals only and have more practical value. Falsetti (1995) used 212 individuals from the Terry Collection to examine metacarpals and found digits 2, 4, and 5 to be applicable to either race. The Terry-based functions were then tested on British ($n = 33$) and New Mexico ($n = 40$) collections. Percentage correct assignments ranged from 58 to 85 percent on the independent samples. The best digits varied among the samples. Although these results fall short of the more encouraging figures of the other workers, they result from the largest samples and most stringent testing. They are surely closer to the practical expectations of casework.

Steele (1976) measured the talus and calcaneus of 239 black and white individuals from the Terry Collection and presented five discriminant functions based on different measurements that correctly assigned sex on the study sample from 79 to 89 percent of the time. France's (1998) discriminant function correctly sexed 132 individuals from her Tennessee Data Base study sample 84 percent of the time.

Miscellaneous Axial Bones   The sternum has probably received more attention than it deserves. The oft-repeated general rule that the manubrium of a male is usually less than half the length of the body, while the manubrium of a female is usually more than half the length of the body has not passed any sort of rigorous testing (see Stewart, 1979a for a discussion). The experience of Jit *et al.* (1980) on a sample from India was that the manubrium–corpus index was not useful. They had more success with a multivariate approach. The glenoid surface of the scapula may be sufficiently dimorphic to be of use, but has not been sufficiently tested. The clavicle appears to have too little dimorphism to serve as a reasonably reliable predictor of sex.

ATTRIBUTION OF SEX FROM THE SKELETONS OF CHILDREN

Assigning sex to immature skeletons has proven more of a challenge than is the case for adults (Weaver, 1998). One might get the impression that for infants and children the probability of error approximates that of a coin flip. The situation is really not that chancy.

Weaver (1980) looked at the iliac auricular surface as a sex discriminator for fetal and infant skeletons; his iliac indices did not prove useful. Three age classes were separately scored for auricular surface elevation: 6–8 fetal months, birth to 1 month, and 3–6 months postpartum. For the fetal sample an elevated surface correctly classified 18 of 24 (75 percent) females and a nonelevated surface correctly placed 22 of 24 (91.7 percent) males. For newborns 54.2 percent of 24 girls had elevated surfaces, and 73.1 percent of 24 boys had nonelevated surfaces. An elevated auricular surface correctly identified 43.5 percent of 23 females, and a nonelevated auricular surface correctly identified 90.6 percent of 32 males of the 6 months group. Attempts to apply these criteria to older children have not so far appeared very successful (Hunt, 1990; Mittler and Sheridan, 1992).

Schutkowski (1987) devised six discriminant functions using combinations of ilium and femur measurements based on data from Fazekas and Kósa (1978) for 43 females and 61 males from 4 to 10 lunar months. Some of the functions had success rates of over 70 percent.

Using a sample of children's skeletons from the Christ Church, Spitalfields, London series that were of known age and sex identified by coffin plates, Schutkowski (1993) identified six morphological skeletal traits that showed significant ($p < 0.05$) sexual dimorphism in children from birth through 5 years. In a sample of 27 boys and 17 girls two mandibular traits segregated significantly with sex: a prominent angular chin was characteristic of boys, while a smooth nonprominent chin was more common in girls; a wide anterior dental arcade characterized boys and a rounded dental arcade was more typical of girls. However, while the angular prominent chin and wide dental arcade characterized 94.1 percent and 82.6 percent of boys, respectively, the morphology typical of girls failed to distinguish girls reliably. The other significant criteria for 29 boys and 22 girls include the following. A greater sciatic notch angle is approximately $90°$ for boys and greater than $90°$ for girls. The greater sciatic notch is deeper in boys and shallower in girls. An "arch" formed by drawing a cranial extension from the vertical side of the sciatic notch crosses the auricular surface in girls, but leads to the lateral rim of the auricular surface in boys. The curvature of the iliac crest when viewed from the top has a faint S-shape in girls and a pronounced S-shape in boys. All four of the iliac traits discriminated the sexes with better than chance reliability, ranging from a high of 95 percent for narrow sciatic notch correctly attributed to boys to a low of 62 percent for a faint S-shape crest belonging to girls.

These criteria test figures reflect only the Spitalfields sample and have not yet been tested for reliability in other samples, so they may reflect a best case scenario. Nevertheless, they are significantly better than a coin flip for young children, and the use of as many of the traits as possible may give the worker a qualitative sense of the level of reliability for an individual sex assessment.

In 2001 Loth and Henneberg examined two other morphological mandibular traits for early childhood sexual dimorphism that had been discerned on a previous survey of 62 known age (birth to 18 years) and sex mandibles from the South African Dart Collection. Male morphology was characterized by a mandibular body shape with a sharply angled transition from the symphyseal region to the lateral body and with a chin extending downward to a pronounced point or squaring off. The female mandibular corpus was gradually curved without an abrupt transition in the symphyseal region and had a chin that was either rounded or gradually tapering to a point. Three workers blindly assessing the 19 Dart Collection individuals aged 4 years or younger accurately assessed sex 89 to 74 percent of the time. A separate test on two South African mandibles and nine French CT scans yielded 82 percent overall accuracy. Loth and Henneberg also reported girls to be more variable than boys.

Here again the estimates of error are likely to be overly optimistic. Interobserver error among those relying solely on the publications for evaluative criteria is not known. The osteology literature presents ample instances of workers having difficulty in perceiving and scoring the standards laid down by others. Two recent cases in point include Loth and Henneberg's difficulty in evaluating Schutkowski's criteria and reproducing his reported accuracy when tested on another sample, and Scheuer's (2002) similar problems when applying Loth and Henneberg's method to the Spitalfields material. The problem appears to be particularly vexatious for remains of the very young. The severe scarcity of well-documented immature skeletons means that testing of methodologies on large independent and diverse samples remains an unrealized ideal. The problem is more pressing for nondental remains. For dental criteria, data taken from living children can often serve as a reasonable proxy for skeletonized remains.

The employment of dental measurements to discriminate the sexes has been applied to the remains of children more often than to remains of adults (Hillson, 1986, 1996). Rösing (1983) measured 55 known sex adults from an old Egyptian cemetery near Aswan. He took four measurements on all the permanent teeth from the first incisors to the first molars of maxilla and mandible: length, width, height of crown, and height of roots. He generated discriminant analyses for 66 different measurement combinations. Of these 66, 16 functions scored 90 percent accuracy; four had 97 percent accuracy for the sample. He could not, however, test on verifiably sexed children from the cemetery.

In 1990 DeVito and Saunders devised discriminant functions to determine sex based on deciduous teeth of Canadian children. These functions correctly classified 76–90 percent of a holdout sample. Combinations of deciduous and permanent tooth measurements classified 83–85 percent of a holdout sample correctly. However, holdout samples from dental clinics are not necessarily indicative of performance in other groups, especially if there are population tooth size differences (Harris and Rathbun, 1991; Saunders, 1992). Indeed, on a population basis, American blacks have larger deciduous and permanent crowns than American Whites (Harris *et al.*, 2001). The functions may be more applicable to modern North American forensic cases, however, than to archaeological remains. It is important to remember that the reliability of standards when applied to different populations and to different age groups than those on which they were devised and tested is essentially unknown. The prudent approach is to make sure that the method employed is ethnically and age group appropriate.

FIGURING THE ERROR RATE

Publications introducing an indicator of sex usually evaluate the criterion by including its success rate on a test population. For example, one might say that the indicator correctly sexed 80 percent of males and 70 percent of females. However, the question being asked of an unidentified individual's remains is: if the indicator is male, what is the chance that the individual it is from is male? The answer is *not* 80 percent sure!

The 1998 Klepinger and Giles paper elaborated the mathematical formulae, based on analogy to the positive and negative predictive values of medical testing, for using a test's success rate in a population to predict its chance for correctly identifying a *single* case as male or female. In practice, however, the formulae are cumbersome and difficult to remember. There is, however, a shortcut to the method and its reasoning. It is very important to understand this difference between performance in a population and performance for an individual case; they are not the same. The former is important for the purposes of paleodemography; the latter is important for forensic anthropology.

Again, a medical analogy may help as a starting place. Suppose that a test for a drug is 95 percent accurate and is applied to a population that has five percent drug users. What is the chance that a person who tests positive is a drug user? Well, about five percent of that population will test positive because they use the drug, and about five percent will test positive because the test is wrong. Therefore, there is a 50 percent chance that a person who tests positive is a drug user. Taking a different emphasis on the same result, there is a 50 percent chance that a person who tests positive is not a drug user. This 50–50 chance is for this specific test in a population that has a prevalence of drug users of 5 percent.

To go back to the indicator of sex example, the same reasoning holds, but now 50 percent of the population is male and 50 percent is female (a.k.a. nonmale). The prevalence of males is about 50 percent. Under these circumstances 80 percent of 50 percent, or 40 percent of the population, will test male because they are male, and 30 percent of 50 percent, or 15 percent, are females who incorrectly test as males. Therefore, 55 percent of the population tests as male, but only 73 percent of those positive male tests are correct ($40/55 = 73$ percent). Likewise, 70 percent of 50 percent (or 35 percent) test female because they are female, and 10 percent of 50 percent of the population are males who falsely test female. Therefore 78 percent of the 45 percent of all positive female tests are from true females ($35/45 = 78$ percent). Assuming the test population and the general population are similar, then if an indicator points to male, the chances are 73 percent that it is correct. If an indicator signals female, there is a 78 percent chance that it is correct.

Since the general population sex ratio is about 1:1, the error rate for the test on any unknown body is the average of the two error rates—in this case $0.5 (27) + 0.5 (22) = 24.5$. Thieme and Schull (1957) put it another way when discussing one of their methods of assigning sex (p. 262): "Suppose now, that an unknown specimen was drawn from the 198 individuals available to us, and we ask how frequently would we misclassify this 'unknown' individual. This frequency would merely be the sum of the products of (1) the probability of drawing a male and the probability of misclassifying him, and (2) the probability of drawing a female and the probability of misclassifying her." The 0.5 in the above equation is the probability of drawing either sex. However, that said, I would emphasize that it is more to the point to state the positive performance for the test appropriate to the sex that the test indicated. In the above example, that would be, say, "the trait (or function) indicated female with a 78 percent probability of being correct." This statement addresses the test performance expectation for this specific individual, not the performance of the test in the long run. For that you could have obtained the same answer by averaging the errors for males and females given in the initial method report, but, to repeat, in forensics the focus is on the single case, not the average accuracy over a population.

To look again at the Klepinger and Giles (1998) examples taken from Weaver's 1980 article on sex differences in fetal and infant auricular surface elevation, an elevated auricular surface as a female indicator correctly sexed 43.5 percent of females and a nonelevated surface correctly sexed 90.6 percent of males. In a population of half males and half females, 43.5 percent of 50 percent (i.e. 21.75 percent of the population) will test female because they are female and 9.4 percent of 50 percent (i.e. 4.7 percent) are males who test incorrectly. The total of female positive tests is $21.75 + 4.7 = 26.45$ percent of the population, and $21.75/26.42 = 0.82$ is the proportion of elevated surfaces that are female. So if the auricular surface is elevated, the probability is 82 percent that it is female.

Likewise, 90.6 percent of 50 percent (or 45.3 percent of the population) with a nonelevated auricular surface correctly test male because they are male, and 56.5 percent of 50 percent (or 28.25 percent of the population) are females who incorrectly test as males. The total percentage of nonelevated surfaces is $45.3 + 28.25 = 73.55$ percent. The proportion of nonelevated surfaces belonging to males is $45.3/73.55 = 0.616$. Thus, a nonelevated auricular surface has a 62 percent probability of being male.

Such results in levels of confidence may seem surprising given the better populational performances for males, but in fact, the higher error rates for the female indicator means that the high number of females who test not female (i.e. male) will swamp the number of true males who correctly test as male. When there is a female indicator, there is much less chance that it is really a male testing incorrectly. Once this reasoning his been mastered it is easily applied to any criterion without having to resort to a more formalized series of steps and equations.

At the risk of being overly repetitive in my proselytizing efforts, I stress that this simple (really) numerical concept is very important in forensic anthropology. It answers the question of the level of certainty for a single unidentified case. The level of certainty is usually different for a female vs a male indication, and the levels of certainly are not the same as success rates on test samples. Note that if an indicator correctly sexes a greater proportion of males than females in a population, then one is more confident of correct sex indication in a single case if the indicator says female. At first glance this may seem counter-intuitive, but the male indicator is more swamped by all those females who are not testing as female.

5

AGE ESTIMATION

Estimation of chronological age from skeletal age in the early years rests on measures of growth and development. Growth is the increase in size. Size increase may be accompanied by a change in form and/or function, which is development. Maturity is the attainment of adult form and function. The age of juveniles is estimated by examining growth and development. Chronological age estimation for adults is based on indicators of aging. "Aging is the universal, progressive, and intrinsic accumulation of deleterious changes" (Kipling *et al.*, 2004: 1426), eventually leading to death. In other words, adult age assessment rests on signs of deterioration. Probably because of more stringent selective pressures, the timing of phases of growth and development is more regular and more synchronized among anatomical sites than is the case for the marks of aging. As a result, the inherent variability in the criteria of assessing biological age progressively increases from fetal life to old age. The degree of uncertainty attached to the age estimate likewise must progress accordingly—the age range that could reasonably encompass the observed morphological stage increases with the age of the deceased. The large age ranges attached to estimates of age for middle-aged and older adults are not so much because the techniques need perfecting as because there is an intrinsic variability in rates of aging that increases dramatically over the life span. This relationship holds at both the gross and microscopic level of observation.

To add to the complexity of estimating age, significant timing differences attributable to sex apply at all of the stages of the life cycle, albeit with varying degrees of magnitude. For adults with reasonably complete skeletons, sex may often be inferred with a high degree of accuracy, but such is not the case for those skeletons that have not yet reached mid-adolescence. Hence for adults sex is frequently known, but the range of age estimation remains comparatively large; for children the age range is comparatively smaller, but the sex is often an unknown. In a way this all seems like some perverse biological version of Heisenberg's uncertainty principle: one cannot simultaneously know with good precision both age and sex.

Anthropological motivation for assessing age at death from skeletal remains arose for the most part from addressing questions revolving around archaeology. The anthropologist/anatomist, often one and the same individual, applied existing criteria and devised new ones in order to investigate the interaction between cultural variables and demographic profiles. The bioarchaeologial focus emphasizes demographic characteristics of past populations, or at least of skeletal series. The individuals who are studied are not really the focus of the analysis, but more like data points to be used in describing a population. In forensic anthropology it is the individuals, not the populations, that are to be characterized. This distinction is not a trivial one when it comes to evaluating systems of estimating age from skeletal remains, especially when the goal is adult age estimation. Age estimation systems devised to serve the goals of paleodemography, even if based on a modern cadaver collection, may involve seriation of individuals in the population by increasing morphological age—not an option in most forensic circumstances. Moreover, demographically oriented techniques focus on 5 or 10 year "modal" age groups with confidence intervals that are rather difficult to estimate. For these reasons, as well as problems with the accuracy of "known", that is, sometimes estimated, ages at death for the Hamann–Todd cadaver collection (Lovejoy et al, 1985a), some skeletal aging methods (Meindl et al., 1985b; Lovejoy et al., 1985b; Walker and Lovejoy, 1985) are inappropriate for most forensic situations.

THE EARLY YEARS

Age estimation for the fetal period and early childhood depends primarily on the appearance and fusion of the major centers of ossification and on the size of various skeletal elements, that is, growth and development. The appearance of ossification centers is very useful in the clinic, but much less so for disarticulated skeletal remains where an element might be missing because it had not ossified, or was too small and undifferentiated in form to be recognized, or was lost postmortem. As a rule it is better to confine attention to what *is* present. Two excellent sources of data on skeletal growth and development in the early years are Fazekas and Kósa (1978) for the fetal period and Scheuer and Black (2000), extending from the fetal period through adolescence. Determination of fetal age most frequently is directed toward the question of whether or not the fetus could have been born alive. From about 3 months on it is largely a matter of size. At 3 fetal months long bones are tubular with no evidence of muscular attachment, and the metopic and mental sutures are unfused. By the end of fetal period the primary centers' individual bones are almost all recognizable. At birth a few secondary centers of ossification, such as the distal end of the femur, are present. There are no carpals and only the calcaneus and talus of the tarsals. The mental suture is beginning to fuse.

Dental Age

Among the age indicators applicable to childhood, dental development and eruption have long been regarded as the gold standard. Tooth development, including both crown and root, has been seen as being less impacted by influences attributable to sex, nutrition, and ill-health than bone growth and development. Dental development has been considered to be so much more tightly tied to chronological age than other skeletal indicators that, in the event of inconsistent estimates from diverse skeletal sites, dental age has been given priority. Discrepancies have then been attributed to the greater effects of environmental variables on bone growth. However, there is reason to regard that assertion with some skepticism, at least as a generalization embracing all ages of childhood (Clegg and Aiello, 1999). Continuing Clegg and Aiello's investigation of discrepancies between dental and skeletal ages and how these track chronological age, Smith (2004) evaluated 6 year longitudinal data for a Montreal sample of 42 boys and 36 girls aged 10–15 years. Among her conclusions was that, "Results from the Montreal French-Canadian sample show that while for a sample of individuals, skeletal and dental ages match reasonably well, there is considerable individual variation among modern children in the timing of skeletal development relative to that of the dentition . . . Nevertheless, a skeletal age in excess of dental age by 2 years or more during adolescence is relatively unusual" (p. 119). A more cautious approach is, if possible, to evaluate many age indicators in arriving at an age interval that includes approximately 95 percent of cases. Nevertheless, studies of dental formation have been more amenable to testing on children of known ages, so the variations are better recognized. For example, dental clinic data analyzed by Harris and McKee (1990) indicated that within each sex, development tended to be advanced in blacks compared to whites, that females tended to advanced development over same aged males, and that this sexual dimorphism in maturation rate was more pronounced in blacks than whites.

The standard for many years was a chart originally published in a 1941 paper by Schour and Massler. The original article does not state the nature and size of the sample observed, but subsequent detective work (Hillson, 1996; Smith, 1991) indicates that, although exact figures remain elusive, the sample was small and based on terminally ill children who died very young. Surprisingly, the Schour and Massler chart in its several reissued versions sold by the American Dental Association does not perform that badly (see Hillson, 1996). The original 1941 chart does not have any quantitative measures of variation at all, although the text of the article refers to considerable variation. Subsequent versions of the chart present plus-and-minus figures, but do not define their meaning. They are certainly not age ranges for each stage and are too small to realistically represent positive and negative standard deviations. The Schour and Massler chart is fairly large, in color, and has easy to distinguish illustrations of primary and secondary teeth. However, for overall quality of data and appropriateness to general forensic use it has been surpassed by the revised chart by Ubelaker (1989) that is reprinted in a larger, more readable format in Buikstra and Ubelaker (1994). Ubelaker constructed the chart using data from several sources, and it is applicable to an ethnically diverse population. The plus-and-minus figures are not the span of two standard deviations because they have been derived from several independent studies, but Ubelaker (1989) states that they cover most of the variation seen for each stage. As with the Schour and Massler chart, the Ubelaker chart combines data from boys and girls because the sex of children's remains is usually not known with any great degree of certainty. The plus-and-minus intervals range from 2 months for fetal and neonate stages to 36 months at age 15. Keep in mind that these age intervals are most appropriate for mostly intact and *in situ* dentitions; when some teeth are missing or loose and hard to specifically identify, the estimated age range should be expanded—by how much is a judgment call.

Another commonly applied standard of dental development is that of Moorrees *et al.* (1963a, b), based on large sample of white children in Ohio. They apply separate standards for boys and girls, and each tooth employed is analyzed separately, so their corresponding two standard deviation intervals are smaller than Ubelaker's intervals. Several stages of tooth formation (crown, root, and apex) are depicted for the following teeth: deciduous mandibular canines, deciduous mandibular molars, permanent mandibular canines, and permanent mandibular molars. Root resorption stages are depicted for deciduous mandibular canines and molars. Each tooth is scored independently and has its own standard deviation for each stage of formation. The more of these teeth that can be used, the better. The large sample sizes and spread statistics are advantages for the method. However, there are some serious hindrances to the practical forensic use of this system. Foremost is that all standards are mandibular; if the mandibular teeth are not present, the system cannot be used, even though maxillary dentition is available. In infants tooth buds may have fallen out of their crypts and may be hard to identify in isolation, although the method is very useful for identifiable loose mandibular molars. For those common circumstances when the sex of the child is not known, Smith's (1991) revision combines the sexes.

Other methods of dental aging (see Hillson, 1996) may be useful in some circumstances. Some workers choose the system of Demirjian and co-workers (Demirjian *et al.*, 1973; Demirjian and Goldstein, 1976) based on a very large sample of French-Canadian boys and girls aged from 2.5 to 17 years. Although it is very large, the sample is ethnically restricted. The authors opine that the patterns of growth will probably not vary that much from one population to another, but that converting the stages to chronological ages may involve a great deal of unknown population variation. Also the Demirjian systems are not that easy to use. The Ubelaker chart is probably the standard of choice for most general usefulness. For full and optimal evaluation, all these methods may require dental radiography in many cases. This may not be possible in some developing countries, but acceptably accurate age estimates can usually be made from gross examination of largely intact dental arcades. Accompanying measures of age variation should be regarded as the measure of precision for the age estimate under the best possible circumstances—in other words, the bare minimum. The usefulness of dental age observations fades after the second permanent molars reach occlusion. Development and eruption of the third molar is so variable that it yields only a very broad estimate of age, made even more broad by any impaction. The final caution is that eruption depicted on charts refers to gingival eruption, not alveolar eruption or occlusion. In the absence of the gingiva, eruption may appear to be more advanced than it really is.

Bone Age

Long Bone Length   Long bone length as an age indicator shares with dental development the advantage of being based on decently large samples of living children of known age. In 1955 Maresh published a longitudinal study that had begun 20 years earlier. One-hundred and seventy-five healthy boys and girls were periodically radiographed from infancy to long bone maturity. Lengths for the six long bones were measured from the radiographs with or without epiphyses (or both ways), as appropriate to age. The measurements are presented as 10th, 25th, 50th, 75th, and 90th percentiles and range for each 6-month age interval. The measurements do have some magnification over true bone length due to parallax, and the amount can vary depending on the bone and the chubbiness of the child—about 2–3 percent would be an average adjustment (Hoffman, 1979). For the lower limbs Anderson *et al.* (1963) followed 50 boys from age 10 and 50 girls from age 8 until epiphyseal union was complete. Half of the children were healthy and half had paralytic poliomyelitis affecting the opposite extremity of the one measured. Amazingly, there were no statistically significant differences in growth at any age between the two series, so the data tables combine the groups. For the most comprehensive coverage of the literature Scheuer and Black (2000) present a large series of tables and regression equations for predicting age on the basis of various long bone and other element measurements; there is an appropriate choice for just about any conceivable occasion.

The above studies plus a few other skeletal growth studies of the midtwentieth century for the most part recorded growth for well-nourished white children. The tempo and timing of growth is influenced by familial, populational, and environmental factors such as nutrition, so the databases of these studies are considerably more constricted than the ethnic and environmental variation encountered in practice. Age-specific yearly increments in growth have almost certainly shifted since these longitudinal studies of long bone length were carried out. The nature and extent of this change remains undocumented and will probably remain undelineated for the foreseeable future. Repeated radiography of healthy children for data gathering purposes can no longer be justified. Even if an imaging procedure that did not have potential deleterious side effects were introduced, the expense of such surveys would put too great a strain on very limited medical resources. Such longitudinal bone growth studies are not apt to be updated to include greater or faster growth fueled by plentiful nutrition. Instead, we may be approaching what has been referred to as the Lake Wobegon effect: All the children are above average. This does not mean that the published tables are invalid or not useful; it simply means that both the means and standard deviations are slightly lower than they should be for twenty-first-century North American children. However, just to emphasize the extent of growth variation, compare the previous sentence with a study by Humphrey (2000), documenting that the femur lengths of known-age children from seventeenth- and eighteenth-century London crypts lay far below the age standards of Maresh's Denver sample. Of course, the Denver sample was living children, and the London sample was children who did not live and presumably died of natural causes; this may account for at least part of the crypt sample growth deficit.

Variability in growth rates of long bone diaphyses has often been regarded as of sufficient extent to render bone length a poor indicator of chronological age, especially compared with dental data. However, Hoffman (1979) has presented data sets based on twentieth-century American girls that bely that generalization. Long bone length and dental *eruption* have comparable variability for the population studied. Dental calcification may have a tighter range of variation than either bone growth or dental eruption, but may not always be available for evaluation. This study suggests that long bone length is an acceptable guide to chronological age up to 12 years.

Union of Primary Ossification Centers   In the skull the anterior fontanelle usually closes in the first 2 years postnatal, and the metopic suture usually closes in the first year, but may not complete fusion for another couple of years, if ever. One should ignore a persistent metopic suture if other age indicators suggest a child older than 2. The inferior portions of the occipital may survive better than the rest of the neurocranium in young children. The lateral portions fuse to the squama between ages 1 and 3, and the basilar portion fuses onto the lateral portions at ages 5–7 (Scheuer and Black, 2000). The two halves of the mandible that are separate at birth fuse at the mandibular symphysis during the first year.

At birth the vertebrae are in three distinct pieces. The halves of the neural arches in the upper lumbar/lower thoracic region begin to fuse in the first year, and this union progresses caudally and cranially. The cervical arches fuse by the early part of the second year and the lower lumbar by the beginning of the sixth year (Scheuer and Black, 2000). The neural arches fuse to the centra between the third and seventh years. In childhood the top and bottom of the centra are quite billowed. Pronounced billowing is characteristic of the bone surfaces abutting growth cartilage and signals active growth during life.

The innominate, or os coxae, is in three parts in infancy. The ischiopubic ramus fuses first between 5 and 8 years of age, but can begin as early as 3 (Scheuer and Black, 2000). The union at the acetabular triradiate cartilage begins at age 10 or 11 and is completed by age 13–15 in females, but may be as late as 17 in males (McKern and Stewart, 1957; Flecker, 1942).

The corpus of the sternum in early childhood comprises four segments. The lower segments may begin to fuse as early as age 4, the middle juncture between 11 and 16, and the upper two fuse by age 20 (Scheuer and Black, 2000).

The sacrum has very complicated primary ossification centers early in infancy (Scheuer and Black, 2000). By age 5 or 6 they have assembled into five separate sacral vertebrae. The lateral elements fuse in early adolescence, then the central portions begin to fuse from the bottom up in late adolescence and early adulthood; the union of S1–S2 may be delayed to as late as age 32 in males (McKern and Stewart, 1957).

For many of the childhood and adolescent years the Tanner–Whitehouse 2 (TW2) method of maturity assessment may be occasionally useful in estimating age. In particular, the more practical version for forensic purposes is the RUS (radius, ulna, short bone) approach (Tanner *et al.*, 1975). Radiographic data for a large sample of British boys and girls were analyzed separately for each sex, and spread was presented as centile curves. The value of TW2 lies not so much in its direct application to forensic remains, but in its delivery of a substantial data set on bone maturation illustrating variation.

Clinical radiographic survey studies (both dental and bone) were designed to serve as standards by which a child of known age could be evaluated on growth and maturity for age. Using the standards to extrapolate chronological age from developmental progress is feasible, but requires some forethought about how variability should be taken into account. Tanner *et al.* (1975: 9) advise about TW2, "Except at the extremes, the curves can also be used to assign a bone age. This is simply the age at which the 50th centile child has the score of the given child." The operative term here is *bone age*, defined as a central tendency measure. Bone age is usually the answer to a clinical inquiry, but is *not* the objective of forensic inquiry. Converting skeletal age to chronological age requires taking the variability factor into account. A 95 percent confidence interval would be nice, if it were known. The standards are usually based on middle-class twentieth-century European-derived populations with known sex. In the larger world of forensic practice the range of normal variation will be greater, but there are no good bases for quantitative estimates. It is better to make your "educated guess" age interval more inclusive than restrictive.

The sex of the deceased child's remains may not be ascertainable with any great degree of assurance, but sex is an important variable in the timing of growth and development. Tanner *et al.* (1975) state that, for their methods, girls are always more skeletally advanced and reach bone maturity about 2 years ahead of boys, on average. For the distal forelimb used in the RUS method, the standard deviation for boys of 5–16 years and girls of 5–14 years was about one year. Krogman (1962), commenting on skeletal maturation in general, proffers the rule of thumb that girls are more advanced than boys by one year between ages 5 and 10, two years between 10 and 15, and again one year between 15 and 20. Within each sex lots of individual variation is normal—as much as 2–6 years depending on the specific site examined. Another source of uncertainty surrounding age estimation in juveniles stems from the recent secular trend towards childhood overweight and obesity. Preliminary clinical evidence suggests that adolescence and maturity are trending towards younger and younger years, and this may be registered in skeletal maturity as well (Klepinger, 2001).

Epiphyseal Fusion   For adolescence and initial adulthood the bony union of secondary centers of ossification to the primary centers is the most useful set of age indicators. Epiphyseal fusion at any particular site does not manifest as a sudden transition from two ossified centers to one. Instead it progresses through a series of stages that can be seen on the gross specimen. Different researchers have different staging schemes, but a summary of McKern and Stewart's (1957) five stages gives a good overview of the fusion process. The initial stage is no bony attachment at all. Then metaphyseal trabeculae begin to cross the growth plate to initiate bony fusion with the epiphysis; this usually begins in the center of the growth plate. Then the epiphysis becomes firmly attached, but there is still a groove left around the periphery of the junction. Eventually a small remnant of the groove can be seen in isolated area. Finally there is no external indication of the growth plate. If you are evaluating closure from a radiograph, be aware that a radiolucent scar may mark the juncture for some time after union is completed. For databases other than McKern and Stewart's (1957) for young men, five stages of epiphyseal closure are more nuanced than the quality of the data demand or even deserve. In most cases the three stages of Buikstra and Ubelaker (1994) are sufficient, especially when translating radiological criteria to direct observation of skeletal material.

In 1942 Flecker published a cross-sectional radiographic study of the appearance and fusion of ossification centers in Australian children of European ancestry. The Flecker group was motivated by what they considered to be serious deficiencies in the very few previous attempts to pin down ages of epiphyseal appearance and maturation. Included here was their dissatisfaction with Stevenson's (1924) paper on epiphyseal union, which was based on small samples, combined males and females into one estimate, and was based on skeletal material from the Hamann–Todd Collection that frequently relied on estimated rather than known age. Flecker's sample sizes vary according to the specific ossification center; males and females are grouped separately. Also Flecker's study is not restricted to the region of the hand and wrist, but includes the centers of the long bones, making it much more applicable to forensically derived skeletal material.

Tables 5.1 and 5.2 present three authors' estimations of the earliest stage of fusion of conjoined epiphyses to diaphyses of the long bones. Flecker's figures come from his group's direct observations. Scheuer and Black's (2000) figures are summaries of their literature survey. Ubelaker (1989) does not state the source of his figures. Also I have taken the liberty of placing the upper end of Ubelaker's age ranges into the completed union table even though they were included in his original table titled "Age of initial union for epiphyses of several bones". Flecker (1942) presents their ages for epiphyseal events in years and months for the youngest and oldest individuals when the months were known from asking date of birth. Flecker's earliest age refers to the age of the youngest individual showing

TABLE 5.1   Age (Years) of Initial Union of Selected Long Bone Epiphyses

Epiphysis	Flecker (1942)		Ubelaker (1989)		Scheuer and Black (2000)	
	Male	Female	Male	Female	Male	Female
Humerus: proximal	16	15 9[a]	14	14	16	13
Humerus: distal	14 7	13 4	11	9	12	11
Medial epicondyle	12	10	15	13	14	13
Radius: proximal	14	13 10	14	13	14	11.5
Radius: distal	17 3	15 11	16	16	16	14
Ulna: proximal	—	11 10	—	—	13	12
Ulna: distal	17 3	15 0	18	16	17	15
Femur: head	14	13 4	15	13	14	12
Greater trochanter	15 10	14 4	16	13	16	14
Lesser trochanter	—	—	15	13	16	16
Femur: distal	16	14	14	14	16	14
Tibia: proximal	16	14	15	14	15	13
Tibia: distal	14 9	13	14	14	15	14
Fibula: proximal	16	14	14	14	15	12
Fibula: distal	15	14 10	14	13	15	12

[a]Read as 15 years, 9 months.

TABLE 5.2   Age (Years) of Completed Union of Selected Long Bone Epiphyses

Epiphysis	Flecker (1942)		Ubelaker (1989)		Scheuer and Black (2000)		McKern and Stewart (1957)
	Male	Female	Male	Female	Male	Female	Male
Humerus: proximal	19 2[a]	20 5	21	20	20	17	24
Humerus: distal	16	16	15	13	17	15	17
Medial epicondyle	17 0	16	18	15	16	15	20
Radius: proximal	20 5	19 10	19	16	17	13	19
Radius: distal	23	20 5	20	19	20	17	23
Ulna: proximal	17 6	16 0	—	—	16	14	19
Ulna: distal	23	22	20	19	20	17	23
Femur: head	20 2	18 2	18	17	19	16	20
Greater trochanter	17 6	16 10	18	17	18	16	20
Lesser trochanter	17 11	16 10	17	17	17	17	20
Femur: distal	19	19	19	17	20	18	22
Tibia: proximal	19	18	19	17	19	17	23
Tibia: distal	18	16 4	18	16	18	16	20
Fibula: proximal	19 8	18	20	18	20	17	22
Fibula: distal	18	16 4	18	16	18	15	20

[a]Read as 19 years, 2 months.

fusion, and completed age refers to oldest individual with no fusion. Thus the criteria for the various authors are not identical. For McKern and Stewart (1957) the completed union age is the lowest age for 100 percent in their final stage, so these ages are older than those of authors using less stringent criteria of epiphyseal fusion. Several workers have pointed out that the long bone epiphyses fall into two groups: earlier fusing and later fusing. The earlier fusing group comprises the elbow, hip, and ankle; the later fusers are shoulder, wrist, and knee. The later fusing group represents sites where most of the growth in the long bones takes place. None of the studies appearing in a literature have a design or sample size amenable to calculating confidence intervals. A reasonable approach is to take wider intervals for the union of any one site and perhaps narrow the final age estimate by looking at as many informative sites as possible and noting where the ranges overlap.

The basilar suture (sphenoid–occipital synchrondrosis) is essentially another example of union of ossification centers. Unlike the bones of the cranial vault that are formed in a process of intermembranous growth, the basioccipital and basisphenoid are, like the long bones, of endochondral origin. Thus the basilar suture shares the same order of fusion time frame as do epiphyses. However, the basilar suture is not amenable to straightforward imaging in the living or observation in the deceased at autopsy, so little is known about the age of fusion. McKern and Stewart (1957) noted that the suture was fused in a majority of young men in the 17–18 year-old age group. It was completely fused in 100 percent of 21year old men. One can only presume that the suture fuses at least a year earlier in females.

The annular epiphyses of the vertebral centra form and fuse in adolescence and early adulthood. McKern and Stewart (1957) presented male fusion data, and Albert and Maples (1995) looked at a small sample of males and females. This particular age marker is as yet not as thoroughly described as other sites maturing at about the same age period.

Timing of the epiphyseal union for the medial end of the clavicle and the anterior iliac crest has been described for a large racially diverse sample of Los Angeles males ($n = 605$) and females ($n = 254$) (Webb and Suchey, 1985). The authors summarize the analysis into handy rules of thumb. For the sternal end of the clavicle, nonunion implies 25 years or less for males and 23 years or less for females; partial union is 17–30 for males and 16–33 for females; complete union implies 21 or older for males and 20 or older for females. For the anterior iliac crest, nonunion suggests 19 or younger in males and 15 or younger in females; partial union is 14–23 in both sexes, and complete union says 17 or older for males and 18 or older for females. This study agrees with the earlier McKern and Stewart (1957) report that the medial clavicle may not completely fuse in males until 31 years.

THE ADULT YEARS

Physiological adulthood roughly comprises the third through the tenth decade. Growth and development taper off to insignificance, followed by ever-increasing signs of skeletal wear and tear that are less dependent on time (i.e. age). That alone leads to less precision in age estimation, only partially mitigated by employing several age criteria. The extent of the potential adult age span adds another and systematic bias to estimates: the strong tendency to overestimate the age of young adults and to underestimate the age of older adults. The trend shows up in all large sample tests of all individual criteria and for multicriteria as well (Molleson and Cox, 1993). The phenomenon described by Masset (1989) for fusion of the cranial sutures applies equally well to the other age markers applicable to adulthood. The inevitable normal individual variation in time (age)-related appearance—which can sometimes range over a scale of decades—is not necessarily expressed as a symmetrical cloud of individual points surrounding a mean value. It is far easier to significantly overestimate than to underestimate the age of a young adult because an underestimation of a decade or so would put the person into the childhood category, which on other grounds is not apt to be confused with adulthood. At the other end of the scale, for persons in their eighth, ninth or tenth decades, errors of underestimation usually fit well into the phases of the original reference sample, whereas age overestimates would have no described standards at all. Only in the middle adult years are the estimation biases likely to go either positive or negative with about equal probability.

Macroscopic Methods

Face of the Pubic Symphysis   Morphological changes to the face of the pubic symphysis have generated more research attention than any other age marker. The history of research on age-related metamorphosis of the pubic symphysis has been reviewed many times (for example, see Stewart, 1979a; Suchey *et al.*, 1984, 1986; Ubelaker, 1989; Meindl and Lovejoy, 1989). Briefly, the first landmark study was T. Wingate Todd's 1920 description of age changes in white males based on 306 skeletons from the Western Reserve University collection now designated the Hamann–Todd Collection. Todd summarized his observations into 10 phases beginning with 18–19 years and ending with the over 50 category. Drawings of Todd's 10 phases of pubic symphyseal metamorphosis somewhat mysteriously circulated some time afterward (Stewart, 1979a) and made their way into various publications. In 1955 Brooks found only 30 percent accuracy when applying Todd's system to the same skeletal collection, and she proposed modifications to improve accuracy.

Two years later McKern and Stewart (1957) presented a different sort of scheme, a three-component evaluation, for predicting the ages of American dead from the Korean War. The sample was entirely male and mostly under the age of 35. The advantage to this approach was that it was based on skeletons of known age at death (as opposed to the Hamann–Todd Collection that included many individuals whose age had been estimated at the time of death) and employed casts that were more revealing of detail than the previous drawings or photos. The major drawbacks included a database sample of 349 young, generally white, men only. Age assignment was based on the total of three individual component scores. The stated age ranges and standard deviations for the total three component score were much too constricted, even for the young adult ages on which it was based. In short, the McKern–Stewart system is simply not reliable enough to be employed in forensic analysis (Klepinger et al., 1992). Meanwhile, in Europe a system of five phases said to be applicable to both males and females was published (Acsádi and Nemeskéri, 1970) as part of an aging system that included cranial suture closure and loss of trabecular bone in the heads of humerus and femur.

However, there was a spreading recognition that a unisex set of standards was not adequate (Brooks and Suchey, 1990). No study of female pubes with a decently large sample size existed, and female symphyseal components did not age in lock step with males—instead some features tended to develop sooner and others later. To address this sexual dimorphism in symphyseal face metamorphosis, Gilbert and McKern (1973) introduced a three-component system based on a sample of 103 females of known age at death. Gilbert recalculated their original statistical table, and the new standard deviations and ranges for the total scores can be found in Suchey (1979) and Ubelaker (1989). Gilbert and McKern (1973) did not include any individuals over 57 years in their analysis sample because they could not discern any regular metamorphic changes after that age.

Perhaps owing in part to the sample size (McKern–Stewart and Gilbert–McKern) or age at death uncertainties (Todd) and in part to observer error, blind tests of the three pubic symphyseal systems on independent samples produced disappointing accuracy (Suchey et al., 1986; Suchey, 1979; Katz and Suchey, 1986). Taking advantage of the availability of pubes from large ethnically diverse samples of males ($n = 739$) and females ($n = 273$) from the Los Angeles County Coroner/Medical Examiner's Office, Suchey and Brooks with statistician Katz devised new male and female systems (Katz and Suchey, 1986; Suchey, 1987; Suchey et al., 1988). In essence the Suchey–Brooks system compresses Todd's 10 phases into six phases for each sex. Each phase is represented by two casts that together illustrate the range of variation for the phase. The accompanying phase descriptions underscore which traits are most important in defining a particular phase. Each phase for each sex has a mean age, standard deviation, and 95 percent range; the 95 percent ranges are not coincident with ± 2 tandard deviations because the research sample ages deviated from a strict normal distribution. Ages at death for all individuals in the sample were verified and ranged from the mid-teens to the late ninth decade. The large age ranges encompassed by all but the earliest phases are conservative estimates of the variation in symphyseal metamorphosis seen in large and diverse populations (Klepinger *et al.*, 1992). The male samples were large enough to refine the phase-specific age estimates according to a three-way white, black, Mexican ethnicity (Katz and Suchey, 1989). Testing of the Suchey–Brooks system on large urban medical examiners' samples (Klepinger *et al.*, 1992) emphasized the disconcerting fact that, for middle-aged and older adults, even the large 95 percent ranges underestimate true variability in symphyseal aging. A test of performance on a sample ($n = 65$) of largely middle-aged and older Asians (Schmitt, 2004) suggested that reliability falls when applied to a population different from the North American urban group on which it was based. Finally, in my opinion female pubes tend to be more difficult to score, presumably because of the extra damage and strain attributable to childbirth.

For forensic analyses the current method of choice would be the Suchey–Brooks system. However, the 95 percent range underestimates the real potential variability. Although the age ranges for more mature symphyses are very large, they can usually be trimmed by examining other additional age markers. The pubic symphyses are one of the more fragile skeletal parts and often stick out in harm's way. If the symphyses have survived intact, almost certainly other informative regions have also.

Sternal Extremity of the Rib   Kerley (1970) noted that the medial end of the ribs, as well as the costal cartilages, underwent morphological changes with increasing adult age, and further investigation was launched by İşcan *et al.* (1984, 1985, 1987), whose initial component study was superceded by phase studies. The first (1984) phase descriptions for the fourth rib were based on 108 white males from the Broward County, Florida, Medical Examiner's Office. The female phase descriptions (1985) were based on a sample of 83 from the same source. Better photos of the eight adult phases for males and females can be found in İşcan and Loth (1986) and Loth and İşcan (1989), and casts of the phases with descriptions (İşcan *et al.*, 1993) can be purchased from France Casting. There are eight phases for both males and females covering ages 14 to the 80s. The original inclusion of tables of descriptive statistics shows that the sample sizes for each phase description vary from a low of $n = 1$ to a high of $n = 18$. The tables also include for each phase a mean, standard deviation, standard error, 95 percent confidence interval and age range. Considering the sample sizes, the statistics are more of an exercise in arithmetic than an indication of the true universe of morphological age variation. By the 1989 and 1993 descriptions, all but the age ranges had been dropped. Nevertheless, given the very small sample sizes the (nonoverlapping) age ranges should be considered to be *minimal* estimates of *unknown* confidence intervals. A further small study (İşcan *et al.*, 1987) suggested that the age progression in blacks differed sufficiently from that of whites to make the white phases of dubious reliability for blacks. Loth and İşcan (1989) report that there is no difference with side and that ribs three and five usually exhibit the same phase as rib four—a useful factoid because ribs four and five are rather difficult to distinguish from each other, especially if in isolation. However, using other ribs does demand caution (Yoder *et al.*, 2001).

The Auricular Surface   The symphysis pubis and sternal rib ends are unfortunately delicate and prone to postmortem damage or destruction. The auricular surface of the ilium is of sturdier stuff and apt to endure harsh circumstances in readable condition longer than the first two. Age changes in the auricular surface in historical review can be found in Lovejoy *et al.* (1985b) and Osbourne *et al.* (2004). The original method was based on observations of large samples, albeit many of the individuals were of unknown age (archaeological) or often estimated age (Hamann–Todd Collection). There were eight phase descriptions of modal ages for nonoverlapping age groups of 5 or 10 years from 20–24 to 60 and more years, accompanied by a series of photographs of only moderate clarity (Lovejoy *et al.*, 1985b; Meindl and Lovejoy, 1989). Each phase was deemed applicable to both males and females unless the latter had well-developed pre-auricular sulci. The application of the method was rather complex and involved seriation, so forensic applications were few. A blind test on the Terry Collection by workers not involved in devising the methodology (Murray and Murray, 1991) found that, indeed, race and sex did not significantly impact the degenerative change. However, they found that the phase age ranges simply understated the variation found in the youngest and especially the oldest age groups. Schmitt (2004) tested the auricular surface technique on the same older Asian sample used to test Suchey–Brooks. In most of this population the method drastically underestimated age—increasingly so for the older ages, and "only 7% of the individuals were accurately classified within five year classes" (p. 3). In independent U.S. Terry Collection and Bass Donated Collection samples correct age classifications (average of 33 percent) for the 5 year phases were improved over the Asian sample, but were still unacceptably high for forensic goals (Osbourne *et al.*, 2004).

In order to address these impediments to forensic serviceability Osbourne *et al.* (2004) used 262 Terry and Bass Collection samples with known age at death to modify the original Lovejoy *et al.* (1985b) method. Amongst the independent variables of collection, sex, ancestry (and combinations of these), and age, only the last showed significant correlation with surface phase indicators. Yet age accounted for only a disappointing 34 percent of the auricular surface variation; other significant contributors to auricular surface degeneration are still unknown. The authors found that collapsing the original eight phases into six and expanding the age ranges for each phase worked as well as a modified eight-phase system. The calculated 95 percent prediction intervals are very much larger than 5 years and comparable to such ranges for the Suchey–Brooks pubic symphysis phases. The new intervals are no doubt also more comparable to the reality of variation. It is not clear whether or to what extent any initial seriation of the sample fits into the procedure. Although the Osbourne *et al.* modification awaits testing on an independent sample, it would appear to be the current better choice for casework.

Cranial Suture Closure   Aside from the endochondral basilar suture, the major sutures of the cranial vault delineate intermembranous bones and lack the more regulated growth and maturation times of cartilaginous growth plates. Forensic interest in this age indicator was stimulated by a series of papers by Todd and Lyon (1924, 1925a–c) on the relationship of age to the progression of endocranial and ectocranial suture closure in black and white males from what is now known as the Hamann–Todd Collection. Masset (1989) reviews the history of investigations into this age indicator. Two of the more commonly used systems have been Acsádi and Nemeskéri's (1970) endocranial phases used as part of their complex method, and Meindl and Lovejoy's (1985) ectocranial phases used as part of their multifactorial method. For both methods the application was targeted at paleodemography. Key *et al.* (1994) tested these two systems and one other on known age individuals from the sixteenth-century London crypt of Christ Church, Spitalfields. They reported great variability in suture closure, so that only broad age categories could be inferred. They found that the more advanced closure of the inner table was mostly complete by age 50 and thereby useful only at ages younger than that. The ectocranial sutures displayed pattern and age variability between males and females. Moreover, they found that open ectocranial sutures could be found in all age groups with about equal frequency and so could not be taken as evidence of youth. To that I add that I have seen a 25-year-old with totally fused sutures and an archaeological series where unilateral suture closure was the rule rather than the exception. I am inclined to disregard cranial suture closure when other age markers can be used. There are, however, occasions when the cranial sutures are all there is, and then the best option is to employ one of Nawrocki's (1998) regression formulae for various combinations of endocranial, ectocranial, and palatine suture closure.

Dental Methods   In 1950 Gustafson developed the first widely recognized technique for estimating adult age from the examination of a single tooth. Six changes associated with age were scored on a 0–3 scale: attrition (occlusal wear), periodontosis (gingival recession), secondary dentin development within the pulp cavity, cementum apposition on the root, root resorption from the apex, and transparency of the apical portion of the root. Some of these characteristics could be seen only microscopically on ground thin sections. The scores for each of the factors were summed and compared with a regression line of total points vs known age for 41 teeth from Swedish dental clinics. For several reasons, including statistical errors, Gustafson's 95 percent confidence interval (± 7.3 years) for predicted ages proved inaccurate. It was much too small.

Maples and his co-workers recognized both the utility of being able to estimate adult age from teeth and the shortcomings of Gustafson's original method, and improved the original formulation by adding variables based on tooth position, race, and sex (Burns and Maples, 1976; Maples and Rice, 1979).

There was, however, another shortcoming to the Gustafson approach and to its various modifications, and that was that it called for the thin sectioning of the teeth. This required some rather specialized equipment, a modicum of training, and partial destruction of the tooth. Lamendin *et al.* (1992) proposed a simpler and nondestructive method for estimating adult age from single rooted teeth. Lamendin's procedure utilized only two dental features that were measured on the labial root surface: periodontosis and root transparency. The latter is better seen when the tooth is placed on a light-table. The resulting equation based on 306 teeth from 208 individuals of known age was:

$$A = (0.18 \times P) + (0.42 \times T) + 25.53$$

where A is age, P is periodontosis height $\times$ 100/root height, and T is transparency height $\times$ 100/root height; heights are in mm. For individuals between 40 and 80 years of age the mean error (the average difference between estimated and actual age) for the Lamendin method (8.9 ± 2.2) was significantly lower than for the revised Gustafson method (14.2 ± 3.4) on a control sample of 39 individuals. The Lamendin method was not recommended for those younger than 40 or older than 80 years because of large errors in the estimate.

The Lamendin *et al.* (1992) study offered a promising option for age estimation for a large segment of the "difficult years" of middle age and older. Nevertheless, questions remained about its general applicability in broad forensic situations. The working and test samples were French-derived, overwhelmingly white, and predominantly male. To investigate the accuracy of the Lamendin technique on a more diverse population, Prince and Ubelaker (2002) sampled the Terry Collection housed at the Smithsonian Institution's National Museum of Natural History: 400 teeth from 94 black females, 72 white females, 98 black males, and 95 white males, aged from 25 to 99 years. For the entire Terry Collection sample the Lamendin technique produced a mean error of 8.23 ± 6.87 years. Once again the mean errors soared for the over 80 set and produced the lowest numbers for the 30- to 70-year olds.

Although the original Lamendin method tested remarkably well on the Terry sample, Prince and Ubelaker (2002) found that accuracy could be improved by modifying the equations to fit the sex and ancestry groups separately. For the new equations the term RH refers to root height; the other terms are the same as the original Lamendin formula. All measurements are in mm.

For black males: $A = 1.04(\text{RH}) + 0.31(P) + 0.47(T) + 1.70$.

The mean error is 6.24 years with a standard deviation of 4.97.

For white males: $A = 0.15(\text{RH}) + 0.29(P) + 0.39(T) + 23.17$

with a mean error of 7.25 ± 5.93 years.

For white females: $A = 1.10(\text{RH}) + 0.31(P) + 0.39(T) + 11.82$

with a mean error of 8.11 ± 6.22 years.

For black females: $A = 1.63(\text{RH}) + 0.48(P) + 0.48(T) - 8.41$

with a mean error of 9.19 ± 7.17 years.

Prince and Ubelaker recommend pre-determining sex and ancestry and using the appropriate new equation when possible.

Although the error terms could be further constricted by limiting the application of the method to those between 30 and 70 years old, this presupposes a knowledge that the analyst does not usually have. In fact, a confidence interval constructed by doubling the standard deviation of the mean error could well miss the actual age for the truly elderly. Other factors to be considered when applying this method are the intra-observer error of 6.5 years (Prince and Ubelaker, 2002) and average inter-observer errors (Lamendin *et al.*, 1992; Prince and Ubelaker, 2002) from 6 to 13 years, some with hefty standard deviations, suggesting that the observation and measurement of the designated features may not be as clear-cut as one might hope.

The Prince and Ubelaker refinement of Lamendin's method for adult dental aging is nondestructive, is reasonably simple in concept and measurement, does not require specialized equipment, and has confidence levels comparable to or better than other methods for assessing the age of mature adults. Although individuals in the Terry Collection were certainly not selected on the basis of excellent oral–dental hygiene, exceptionally poor hygiene could certainly accelerate the rate of periodontosis in particular and should be considered in cases where there is evidence of long-standing neglect. This technique would not be appropriate to evaluating dental age from habitual users of methamphetamine who display "meth mouth".

Microscopic Methods

Ellis Kerley pioneered the histological approach to the determination of age in human bone. Kerley's original (1965) work exploited the ontological patterns of change in the microscopic structures of cortical bone from youth to old age. Undecalcified thin cross sections of the midshafts of long bones of the leg were examined under 100-power fields of a light microscope. Four microscopic fields for each section—anterior, posterior, lateral, and medial—were placed to abut the outer, or periosteal, surface. Within each of the four fields the number of osteons (or Haversian systems), osteon fragments, and non-Haversian canals were counted, and the percentage of the field occupied by circumferential lamellar bone was estimated. The first three numbers were summed across the four fields, and the percentage of circumferential lamellar bone averaged to give a summary picture of the cross section. Each of these summary values was plotted against known age at death. Because of the continuous microstructure remodeling of cortical bones, old bone—both osteonal and circumferential lamellar—is partially resorbed and replaced by new osteons in a somewhat altered position. With increasing age the number of osteons increases, as does the number of osteon fragments, which represent the remnants of remodeled osteons. The circumferential lamellar bone is laid down rapidly with the growth of youth, but the deposition rate slows markedly in adulthood. As the circumferential bone becomes remodeled to osteonal bone, its percentage of the field shrinks, but because of some continuing deposition, never quite disappears. The number of non-Haversian canals found in the circumferential bone also decreases with advancing age and eventually disappears around age 55.

Regression formulae, either linear or curvilinear, for each plot of a feature (e.g. femoral osteons, tibial fragments) vs age were calculated. The regression formulae were revised by Kerley and Ubelaker (1978), and the new standard errors of the estimates ranged from a high of 14.62 years for fibular non-Haversian canals to a low of 3.66 years for fibular osteon fragments. While the fibular fragments are clearly the feature of choice, if that is not a choice that can be made, other structures with acceptably low standard errors are femoral fragments (6.98), fibular osteons (8.33), tibial fragments (8.42), and femoral osteons (9.19).

Other variations of the Kerley method have been published, and these are reviewed in Stout (1989, 1992). Suffice it to say here that none have proved to be clearly more appropriate for forensic use. Stout (1986; Cho *et al.*, 2002) has extended the microscopic analysis to the rib cross section, and that may come in handy under some circumstances.

The microscopic methods clearly have some disadvantages. They are destructive of bone, and although this is not extensive, it still requires permission. The methods require equipment for sectioning, grinding, and mounting bone, and an inexpensive light microscope. A bigger technical hurdle is that some hands-on training with an experienced practitioner is necessary to achieve the levels of accuracy expected. Even in situations where all the recovered bone is fragmentary, the microscopic approach may not be applicable. The cortex of the bone must be intact and undamaged. Do not be seduced into believing that investigators or jurors will find laboratory scientific findings to be inherently more persuasive than macroscopic observations. If they do not understand the principles of bone histology, they are just as likely to dismiss the analysis altogether as to accept it on blind faith. Guiding the lay public is more challenging for the histological methods. On the positive side microscopic methods can be applied to small sections of lower limb or rib that may be recovered when the specific skeletal sites of other age markers have not.

How do macroscopic and microscopic methods of age estimation compare as to accuracy and general applicability? Of course, each age marker tends to have its quirks and fortes, but in general the two types of analyses are quite comparable. The approximate 95 percent confidence intervals, when known, are comparable for similarly aged adults, although some techniques such as dental aging may have the edge over a substantial span of middle adulthood. Those techniques for which confidence intervals are not known or even closely approximated should not be relied upon unless all else fails. Aiello and Molleson (1993) have investigated some of these comparison questions on the Spitalfields sample and found that histological aging based on one population does not necessarily translate accurately to individuals of another population—just like the macroscopic techniques. They also stated that, "The important point to realize is that all of the techniques, including the histological techniques, are reflecting the age structure and/or conditions of the reference populations upon which they were developed" (p. 702). They also point out that, for the same individual, agreement between macro-scopic and microscopic techniques does not guarantee their accuracy. Dudar *et al.* (1993) evaluated two adult age at death methods using documented historical cemeteries and anatomy laboratory cadavers. Specifically, they used sternal rib ends and osteons of rib cortex. Like other methods both tended to overage younger adults and underage older adults. An average of the two age estimates produced the best regression line ($r = 0.86$) and the smallest standard error of the estimate (7.5 years). [This is probably a good place to point out once again that the confidence intervals for regression lines are not linear and that only for the more central portion of the line does ± 2 times the error of the estimate approximate the 95 percent interval.]

Other Age Indicators

The techniques of age estimation discussed thus far are those that have received the most attention in the literature and in casework because they are based, to greater or lesser extent, on known age research samples. In addition, most have undergone blind testing on independent samples of known age at death and have some sort of age ranges attached to progressive morphological phases. There are other more qualitative signs of broad age categories (Kerley, 1970).

Skeletal changes that accompany advancing age often begin unobtrusively, but may advance to outright pathology. Joint wear and tear is a case in point. In young adults the joint margins are rounded, but with advanced age a cuff of bone forms around the margins of the joints. Osteophytes (spurs) form in the vertebral column and where tendons or ligaments attach. Because vigorous physical activity and injury can hasten the appearance of these outgrowths they are suggestive guidelines at best and must be approached cautiously.

Advanced age is characterized by resorption of cancellous bone throughout the skeleton (for an overview see Sorg *et al.*, 1989). The head of the humerus has received the most attention in attempts to scale radiographic evaluation of bone loss, but only as part of a multi-indicator method. Senile osteopenia/osteoporosis is also notable in the proximal femur, vertebrae, and even the cranial vault where loss of diploë and marrow in the parietal can thin and flatten the area superior to the temporal lines. With advancing age, bone resorbs along the medullary cavity of long bones. Circumferential subperiosteal new bone is also laid down, but more slowly than medullary resorption. Consequently, there is net bone loss with increasing bone and medullary cavity diameter. The combination of medullary and trabecular bone loss renders the bones almost feather-like in weight by advanced old age. Bone resorption accelerates with physical inactivity, which often accompanies old age, but may also characterize younger individuals. Disuse atrophy of the disabled can usually be distinguished from senile osteoporosis in active elders. In the latter there is medullary thinning, but areas of muscular attachment maintain their definition. In disuse atrophy there is diminution of the muscular attachments and resorption throughout the cortex, including the subperiosteal region. Therefore, the age of such specimens cannot be determined microscopically.

Several areas of cartilage tend to ossify with advancing age. Included here are the xyphoid process of the sternum, the thyroid and cricoid cartilages, and costal cartilages. Fusion of the sacroiliac joint, usually unilateral, is not uncommon in old men. However, sacroiliac fusion may also occur as an initial sign in young men with ankylosing spondylitis. The sacroiliac of women does not fuse, but can show ligamentous bone spurs.

CONCLUDING REMARKS ON ADULT AGE ESTIMATION

As many have already stated, it is best to employ as many techniques as possible and appropriate. However, this is not a fixed suite of procedures, but a guideline that emphasizes the circumstances of the case, including assessments of sex and ancestry, as well as any overall clues as to whether the individual is of young, middle, or old adulthood. "Flyers", that is, age estimates way out of line with other estimation methods, can only be detected using more than one or two markers. Flyers can affect one or two sites because the more or less continual microtrauma of normal life can be overwhelmed by one or a few incidents of higher degree trauma.

Although the use of multiple age markers can also help to narrow down an approximate 95 percent confidence interval, that interval will still be on the order of 15–20 *at best* once all the sources of uncertainty, such as inter- and intra-observer errors, are taken into account. This sort of imprecise estimate is exasperating for all involved in the investigation, but when trying to identify unknown remains it is far better to be approximately correct than to be precisely wrong.

6

DECIPHERING ANCESTRAL BACKGROUND

THE BIOLOGICAL AND THE CULTURAL

For biologists and anthropologists, the traditional concept of race as a classification of populations with roots in typology is dead. The corpse of the typological concept deserves a cursory examination, or, to paraphrase Kennedy's (1995) rhetorical question: if races do not exist, is trying to identify them an exercise in *non sequitur*? Not really.

Society at large uses racial and/or ethnic classifications for a variety of purposes including, for example, affirmative action, marketing, and missing persons descriptions. Racial attribution can be a useful datum in ascertaining personal identity from human remains and, sometimes just as useful, in excluding a putative candidate from a list of possible identifications. Ancestry and ethnicity are terms that have sometimes (often) been applied simply as a gloss for the term race in hopes of avoiding all the negative baggage the term "race" carries along with it, but they are not really synonymous, even in the vernacular. Ethnicity is a cultural term that conflates poorly with an individual's geographical ancestral origins. "Hispanic" is a case in point. The term can refer to so many different ancestral origins and combinations thereof that its correlation to phenotypic traits approaches nil in many regions. It is argued here that "ancestry" most closely approximates the type of assessment that forensic anthropologists can hope to

Fundamentals of Forensic Anthropology, by Linda L. Klepinger
Copyright © 2006 John Wiley & Sons, Inc.

operationally arrive at. The term does not force a false exclusivity of classi-fication; it allows consideration of diverse background contributions, albeit in a limited way.

There is no getting around the fact that medical–legal investigators of all stripes expect forensic anthropologists to at least address the question of a racial characterization in cases of attempts to identify unknown remains, even if that is to report unsuccessful efforts to reach a conclusion. Refusal to acknowledge the existence of any observable populational biological differences will not be well received. Moreover, such ancestral information is undeniably helpful in the search for an identity. Therefore, to react to the term race (or ancestry) as a vampire to sunlight is counterproductive.

The Biological Context

Genotypic and phenotypic variations among human populations are both geographically and culturally structured. A recent analysis (Rosenberg *et al.*, 2002) of human genetic population structure revealed that inter-individual differences within populations account for 93–95 percent of genetic variation and that differences among major population groups account for only 3–5 percent. The vast majority of alleles are worldwide in distribution; private alleles, or alleles restricted to one group, are very rare. Nevertheless, when allele frequencies were clustered into five groups, the resultant groups corresponded to the world's major geographic regions: Africa, Eurasia (Europe and West, Central, and South Asia), East Asia, Oceania, and the Americas (see also King and Motulsky, 2002). More-over, there was excellent agreement between individuals' membership in the clusters and their self-reported regions of ancestry.

The situation for osteologists is not so straightforward because we are not analyzing DNA, but skeletal traits of uncertain heritability. Heritability is the proportion of phenotypic variation that is attributable to genetic variation. Insofar as phenotypic trait diversity reflects genetic diversity, we can expect at least some suite of these traits to also cluster according to geo-graphic ancestry. Because of the added level of unknown heritability, however, successful correspondence between clusters and ancestry will fall short of that achieved by geneticists.

The Cultural Component

Added onto this, the forensic anthropologist faces another level of potential pitfalls: the translation of biological data into the dominant societally con-structed categories that do not reliably coincide with biological clusters (see Gill, 1998 for discussion). For instance, the Eurasian geographical group may be glossed as "Caucasian", but many people in the general population who are involved in medical–legal investigations would not include South Asians in the "Caucasian" category. Very few forensic anthropologists are capable of making reliable ethnic distinctions, such as Indian, within the large group, so it is incumbent on the analysts to explain in a report that a racial or ancestral category may be very inclusive. Another interpretation problem arises from the fact that not all ancestral contributions are equally considered in social classifications; African ancestral contributions often take precedence over others that constitute equal or greater percentages.

SKELETAL INDICATORS

Human remains that have undergone heavy decomposition, as well as skeletal remains, are heavily dependent on skeletal traits for estimation of ancestry. As decomposition progresses, the skin changes color in a variety of ways that serve to overwhelm and disguise the complexion of the individual during life. Head hair, however, can be very useful—especially in children where modifications of natural form and color are rare.

Certain skeletal characteristics do appear with greater frequency in some geographical populations than in others. Because none of these traits is a "marker" for population affiliation, many traits must be considered in the tally that suggests the predominant ancestral population contribution(s). The skull is by far the most informative region because that is where the variant traits concentrate. In North America the most studied groups are American Caucasians (whites), African-Americans (blacks), and East Asian/Amerindians, the last group heavily influenced by the Native Americans. The following discussion centers on those divisions.

The Skull

Not all racially variable morphological traits are equally useful or equally easy to assess. Some traits that show statistically significant population differences are not very meaningful on a single individual because the trait frequencies in different populations are not that all that different. Some of the traits that occur with different frequency among ancestral groups also vary in expression according to sex, so skeletal indicators of sex should first be taken into consideration. Age is also a factor. The discussion here refers to adult skulls. However, some traits can be found on children older than infancy.

Tables 6.1–6.3 list 25 traits that tend to typify Caucasians, African-Americans, and Asian/Amerindian geographic groups. The lists of skeletal

TABLE 6.1   Some Skull Traits Characteristic of Caucasians

1. Inion hook often pronounced
2. Marked depressions for longus capitus insertions
3. Long base chord
4. Receding frontal profile
5. Metopism occasional
6. Metopic trace (remnant) frequent
7. Inca bone rare
8. Orbits sloping downward laterally
9. Depressed nasion (nasal root)
10. Tower nasals
11. Elevated nasal bridge
12. Projecting nasal spine
13. Nasal sill pronounced and sharp.
14. Long narrow nasal aperture
15. Retreating zygomatics
16. Little or no lower facial prognathism
17. Oval window visible through round external auditory meatus
18. Major sutures simple
19. Parabolic dental arcade
20. Bulging palatine suture with dip at midline
21. Prominent chin
22. Undulating inferior mandibular border
23. Pinched ascending mandibular ramus
24. Carrabelli's cusp on maxillary first molar frequent
25. Lingual incisors usually spatulate

attributes are by no means complete and definitive. Traditional popularity and my personal preferences—or at least my ability to understand the nature of the trait—influence the lists. Some of these traits are indicated by their numbers in Figures 6.1–6.3 respectively. The traits listed and illustrated for the Asian/Amerindian group are generally specific to Native Americans of the southwestern United States, who are best represented in the literature. East Asians typically express many of these traits, although sometimes to a different degree. Figures 6.4 and 6.5 show three males of the Asian/Amerindian group. The nasal bridge of many Native Americans is more elevated than that of East Asians, although there is a great deal of variation across regions of the Americas. Some traits, as the shovel-shaped incisors (Fig. 6.6), are very frequent in both groups.

Another example of the typical variability encountered within one of the geographical groups is illustrated in Figure 6.7. The two crania of African-American males differ in several respects, but certainly do not represent the extreme range of variation that can be seen among those identified by themselves and others as African-American.

TABLE 6.2   Some Skull Traits Characteristic of African-Americans

1. Long, low, narrow cranial vault
2. Post-bregmatic depression
3. Long base chord
4. Rounded forehead
5. Major sutures simple
6. Vascular markings on frontal bone common
7. Low and wide (more square) orbits
8. Broad interorbital distance
9. "Quonset hut" nasals
10. Little nasal root depression
11. Broad, low nasal bridge
12. Wide nasal aperture
13. Small nasal spine
14. Guttered lower nasal border (sulcus), sill rare
15. Somewhat retreating zygomatics
16. Alveolar prognathism
17. Oval window visible through round external auditory meatus
18. Hyperbolic (rectangular) palate
19. Bulging palatine suture
20. Straight inferior mandibular border
21. Medial cant to posterior border of ascending ramus
22. Spatulate lingual incisors
23. Carrabelli's cusp rare
24. Crenulated molar cusp pattern
25. Frequently two to three lingual cusps on lower first premolar

A much more startling example of intra-population variability is seen in Figure 6.8. The crania of an older adult male and an adolescent female from the same prehistoric Midwestern archaeological site show much greater variation than one would expect in relatively sedentary village people. If seen in a forensic rather than archaeological context, a significant African-American ancestral contribution would be assumed for the female. Interestingly, this same male/female difference is found in other individuals and in other sites from the same general area, so it is not an isolated fluke.

One trait that shows high frequency only among Polynesians is "rocker jaw". The inferior border of the horizontal mandibular ramus forms a long convex curve. Consequently, when the mandible is set (in anatomical position) on a table, it easily rocks back and forth like a rocking chair. This trait among Polynesians has a frequency of about 70–80 percent (Houghton, 1977). The trait may also appear in low frequency in Native Americans.

Recently, Edgar (2005) has explored the usefulness of eight dental traits in various combinations in predicting Caucasian vs African-American identity.

TABLE 6.3   Some Skull Traits Characteristic of Asians/Amerindians

1. Rounded (spherical) vault
2. Short base chord
3. Major sutures complex with frequent wormian (sutural) bones
4. Inca bone occasionally
5. Sagittal keeling of vault common
6. Vertical frontal profile
7. Depressed glabella frequent
8. Tented nasals
9. Rounded orbits
10. Narrow nasal bridge with nasal crest frequent
11. Nasal overhang (especially in southwestern Amerindians)
12. Nasal aperture rounded and medium wide
13. Inferior nasal spine moderate and nasal sill indistinct
14. Prominent flared zygomatics with inferior projection
15. Posterior process (tubercle) on zygomatics
16. Moderate to no alveolar prognathism
17. Elliptic (horseshoe-shaped) dental arcade
18. Straight palatine suture
19. Buccal alveolar ridging
20. Oval window not visible through elliptic external auditory meatus
21. Straight inferior mandibular border and wide ascending ramus
22. Everted gonial angle
23. Shoveling of lingual incisors
24. Enamel extensions onto roots frequent
25. Molar buccal pits common

On an independent test sample of 40, the method predicted correctly 90 percent of the time, so it is certainly promising. The method is, however, more suitable for the advanced worker than for the beginner. Along similar lines, Lease and Sciulli (2005) report similar success in assigning Caucasian and African-American children to correct ancestral groups on the basis of morphology and metrics of deciduous teeth.

How to score the morphological traits is not always straightforward, and idiosyncratic traits are fairly common. Moreover, there is the inevitable mix in one individual of traits suggestive of more than one ancestral group, but weighting of traits for discriminating power is not explicit. Inexperienced workers may be justifiably dubious about the strength of their conclusions. The need for a more objective means of assigning ancestry prompted Giles and Elliot (1962) to devise a three-way discriminant function analysis to place an unidentified cranium into the white, black or Amerindian camp. Two equations were required for eight measurements, and these two equations differed according to sex. For each sex there was a scaled chart with a three-way division onto which the two formulae calculations were

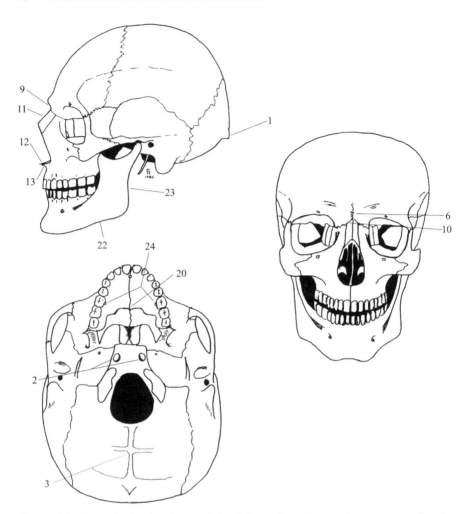

Figure 6.1 Some skull traits characteristic of Caucasians. The numbers correspond to the numbers in Table 6.1. Modified from Rhine (1990) by permission of Maxwell Museum of Anthropology.

plotted to assign the most likely racial group. The closer a point was to a dividing line, the less strong the discrimination was between the groups on either side of that line. The database for deriving the formulae was 75 each white, black and Indian males and females. The Indian sample was from Indian Knoll, an Archaic site from Kentucky. Large, and largely Indian, male and female test samples not used in the computations were correctly classified 82.6 percent of the time for males and 88.1 percent of the time for females. Snow *et al.* (1979) "field tested" the Giles and Elliot equations on 52 complete skeletons of known sex and race drawn from

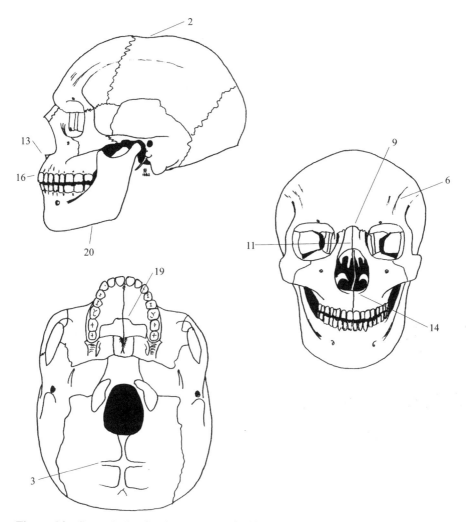

Figure 6.2   Some skull traits characteristic of African-Americans. The numbers correspond to the numbers in Table 6.2. Modified from Rhine (1990) by permission of Maxwell Museum of Anthropology.

Snow's casework in Oklahoma. The functions correctly diagnosed blacks and whites 83 percent of the time, but misclassified six of seven Native Americans in the series. They surmised that the Indian Knoll sample did not represent well contemporary American Indian populations. For those with PC systems, FORDISC 3.0 offers discriminant functions for the three dominant North American groups. Gill *et al.* (1988) devised a metric technique for separating Native Americans from whites on the basis of the mid-facial skeleton. However, the method requires the use of a simometer, a

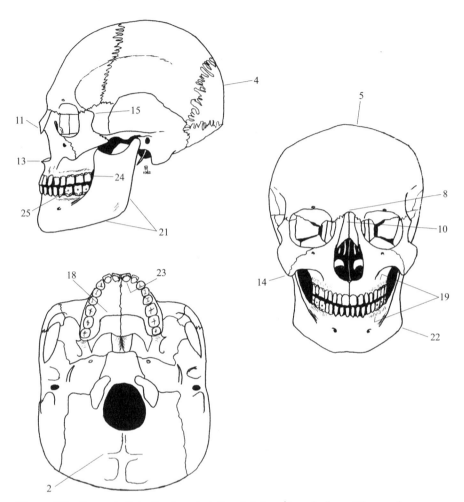

Figure 6.3 Some skull traits characteristic of Asians/Amerindians. The numbers correspond to the numbers in Table 6.3. Modified from Rhine (1990) by permission of Maxwell Museum of Anthropology.

coordinate caliper modified with angled points that can be brought to a common point and used to take small measurements.

While the discriminant function approach offers greater objectivity in the analysis, it cannot solve all the problems associated with assessing ancestry. Individuals of mixed-race ancestry will still often fall close to the sectioning lines. All of the measurements cannot be assumed to be independent and uncorrelated with the others. Consequently, 10 measurements may not be analogous to 10 morphological traits, which may not be independent either. There are not that many measurements, and they need to be taken on skulls that preserve the original adult measurements. For example, an

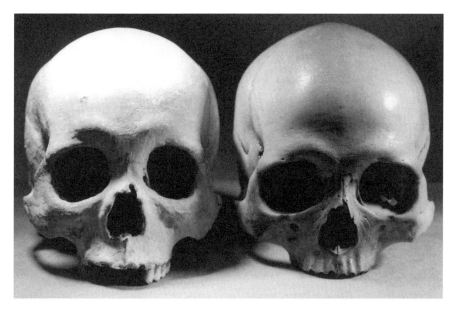

Figure 6.4   Crania of two East Asian males.

Figure 6.5   Crania of East Asian (left) and North American Amerindian (right). Both are males.

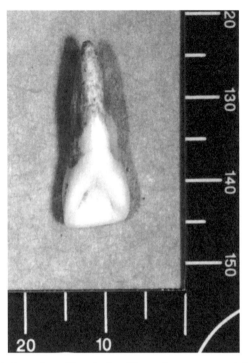

Figure 6.6 Lingual view of maxillary incisor illustrating pronounced shoveling and enamel extension onto the root. Mandibular incisors generally display only slight to moderate ridging along the mesial and distal sides.

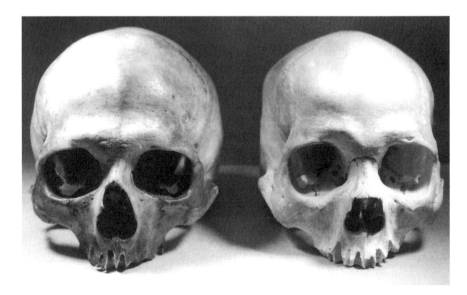

Figure 6.7 Crania of two African-American males.

Figure 6.8 Crania of adolescent female (left) and older adult male (right) from the same midwestern archaeological site.

edentulous skull with alveolar resorption may give spurious results. So, with metrics or morphology, professional opinion stills plays an important role. Discriminant functions should not serve as recipes for "the" definitive answer; all the observable features of a skull should be taken into account when deciding upon ancestry. There are cases that appear to be a melange of the world's geographical attributes, and a definitive conclusion is not warranted. At these times it is good to remember Voltaire's dictum, "Doubt is not a pleasant condition, but certainty is an absurd one."

The Postcranium

In encountering recovered remains lacking the skull, it may be possible to estimate ancestry if there is a femur. Stewart (1962; also see Bass, 1995) investigated the anterior curvature of the diaphysis and degree of torsion of the proximal femur. The femora of African-Americans tend to be flat; that is, they have less anterior bowing. Generally femora of Asian/ Amerindians tend toward the greatest anterior bowing, and those of Caucasians fall in between. Asian-Amerindians tend towards the greatest anteversion of the femoral head and angulation of the femoral neck; African-Americans tend to have the least torsion.

Gilbert and Gill (1990) reported that anterior–posterior flattening of the proximal femur just below the lessor trochanter (platymeria) was more pronounced in American Indians than in American blacks or whites. Recently Wescott (2005) investigated the platymeric index, a measure of anterior–posterior femoral flattening, in samples of Native Americans, Polynesians, Hispanics, American whites, and American blacks. The largest sample was historic and prehistoric Native Americans ($n = 1659$), and the smallest was Hispanics ($n = 41$) from the Forensic Data Base. He found that the shape of the anterior subtrochanteric shaft was useful in separating the relatively flat proximal femoral profiles of Native Americans and Polynesians from American whites and blacks, who had rounder subtrochanteric regions. Interestingly, the platymeric index did not separate Hispanics from blacks and whites. However, the Hispanic sample was small and of unknown national origin. The two platymeric samples, Native American and Polynesian (Hawaiian), were from largely archaeological populations that had very different activity patterns and activity levels from the other three sampled groups that were all modern. The extent to which habitual activities modify any genetic contributions to proximal femur shape has yet to be determined.

There is also a tendency for African-Americans to have greater intercondylar notch height (viewed from the distal end) than American Caucasians (Baker et al., 1990). This appears to hold for both sexes. The method has not, to my knowledge, been tested on a large independent sample. Examination of the intercondylar shelf angle (Craig, 1995) is another approach using the distal femur.

The ratio of distal limb bone length to proximal limb bone length is statistically significantly greater in African-Americans than in the other groups, but useful in the individual case only if the trait is pronounced. Multiple discriminant function analysis of the femur and innominate has been applied to the simultaneous assignment of sex and race (DiBennardo and Taylor, 1983).

Because there are fewer traits to score on the postcranial skeleton, and because many of them have greater overlap among groups than cranial traits, one's level of confidence in ancestral assignment is lower and even harder to quantify than levels of confidence based on skull analysis.

7

STATURE ESTIMATION

It was a dark and stormy night when the professor went missing, in fact, election eve, 1992. After a few days, descriptions of the missing professor and his car appeared in two local newspapers, and his family and friends circulated a flier. The flier listed the professor as 5 foot 9 inches, while both newspapers reported him to be 5 foot 7 inches. Discrepancies in height attributions are not unusual, and all recorded statures for a person may vary from dead wrong to approximately correct. We will never know. After the snow melted he was found drowned in a retention pond; his car had slipped into the pond while he was turning around in a rural driveway that was the wrong address for the party he had planned on attending.

HOW TALL ARE YOU, REALLY?

Giles and Hutchinson (1991) have reviewed the major sources of extraneous variation in attempting to determine a "true" stature. These include average variations of nearly an inch attributable to the time of day; gravity pulls down on the vertically oriented during the course of a normal day. The measurement technique and variation among measurers introduce inaccuracies from half a centimeter to several centimeters—the greater errors usually attributable to medical, police, or correctional personnel untrained in

Fundamentals of Forensic Anthropology, by Linda L. Klepinger

measurement techniques. Trained measurers using freestanding anthrop-ometers on shoe-less subjects achieve the greatest accuracy and reproducibil-ity in measurements, and even then small variations persist.

Noticeable inaccuracies in recorded heights of the living can result from systematic biases to random errors to simple over-optimism. Willey and Falsetti (1991) in a study of over 500 primarily young adults discovered stat-istically significant overestimation of driver's license stature compared with measured stature. They also saw a tendency in males to round up to even inches on driver's licenses. Driver's license data are often used as a source of antemortem descriptions.

Analyzing a very large U.S. Army database (6669 males and 1330 females) for young adults, Giles and Hutchinson (1991) compared self-reported and uniformly measured stature. They found that over the entire range of height males, on average, overestimated their stature by about 2.5 cm (1 inch), and women over-reported by an average of about 1 cm ($\frac{3}{8}$ inch). Shorter men tended to over-report to a somewhat greater extent than taller men, but on average all over-reported their stature to some degree; no height categories under-reported.

These two studies are consonant in reporting the tendency of young adults to overestimate their height, men on average to a greater extent than women. Can this phenomenon be simply attributed to an over-exuberance of youth that becomes more restrained and realistic as maturity progresses? *Au contraire.*

The loss of stature that attends adult aging becomes quite noticeable in the elderly, but begins earlier. Age-related bias exacerbates the inaccuracy of self-reported stature. Giles and Hutchinson (1991) found that men 45–54 years of age over-reported their stature by an average of 0.25 cm ($\frac{1}{8}$ inch), in the following decade by 0.6 cm ($\frac{1}{4}$ inch), and between 65 and 74 by 1.25 cm ($\frac{1}{2}$ inch)—in addition to the overestimate expected of younger men. The effect for women was an additional over-reporting of 0.5 cm ($\frac{1}{4}$ inch) between 45 and 54, 1.2 cm ($\frac{1}{2}$ inch) between 55 and 64, and 2.5 cm (1 inch) for those 65–74. These biases are important to consider in establishing an estimate of living stature and in the estimation of stature from long bone length.

ESTIMATION OF LIVING STATURE FROM SKELETAL REMAINS

Stewart (1979a) reviewed the historical highlights of stature estimation from postmortem remains. Several efforts were proffered in the nineteenth century, but North American studies are a feature of the twentieth century, a time when European methods and European population applications expanded, and numerous estimation equations for various Asian populations appeared in the literature (Krogman and İşcan, 1986). Regression formulae for circumscribed European or Asian populations can certainly be the method of choice in circumstances where the corresponding ethnicity of the deceased is known and appropriate to the chosen formula. However, here we will focus discussion on those methods most applicable to the general North American adult population. One of these methods was devised in Europe.

The Fully Method

In 1956 Georges Fully, a French physician, published a method for estimating stature from skeletal remains that improved upon the European methods of the day (Stewart, 1979b). Fully's "anatomical" method incorporated measurements of skeletal elements from head vertex to heel (Fully, 1956). The method is based on data from a very large sample of skeletons exhumed from a German concentration camp after World War II and for whom identity and measured height at arrival could be determined. The original article is rather hard to come by, but the method and measurements are described in Lundy (1988) and Stewart (1979a). In brief,

height = basion-bregma height + maximum heights of vertebral bodies
C2 through S1 + lengths of femur (bicondylar) and tibia (maximum omitting spines) + articulated height of talus and calcaneus + soft tissue factor

The correction factor for soft tissue was assigned by three categories:

If calculated stature is 153.5 cm (60.5 inches) or less, add 10 cm (4 inches)
If 153.6 − 165.4 cm (60.5 to 65.1 inches), add 10.5 cm (4.1 inches)
If 165 cm (or 65 inches) or greater, add 11.5 cm (4.5 inches)

The correction factor can also be stroked somewhat to take age or vertebral pathology into account. The method recommends articulating the spinal column beforehand in order to detect abnormal curvatures or other pathologies. If, for age or other reasons, there is kyphosis or scoliosis, then one measures minimum as well as maximum vertebral body height and takes the average of these measurements. Thus the technique accounts for a significant portion of aging stature loss.

The simple summation of measurements does not generate a standard error of the estimate, but the specific individual errors of the estimate were astonishingly small. For the entire sample including 42 new cases, more than 80 percent of calculated statures differed from the known stature by less than 2 cm. There were no errors exceeding 3.5 cm.

An obvious shortcoming of the anatomical method is that it requires a largely complete and undamaged skeleton. In 1960 Fully and Pineau published a second version that allowed calculation of stature when the skull and some vertebrae were missing (see also Stewart 1979a). This second study was based on the skeletons of 164 identified men between the ages of 18 and 65 years and between 151 and 188 cm tall. Two of the more useful regression equations follow.

$$\text{Stature} = 2.09 \, (\text{femur} + 5 \text{ lumbars}) + 42.67 \pm 2.35 \, \text{cm}$$
$$\text{Stature} = 2.32 \, (\text{tibia} + 5 \text{ lumbars}) + 48.63 \pm 2.54 \, \text{cm}$$

The standard errors of the estimate are generally smaller than for stature regression formulae based on long bones alone, which is not surprising considering that more measurements that contribute to height go into the Fully and Pineau (1960) estimates. Fully and Pineau remark that the two major components of stature, trunk length, and lower limb length are only weakly correlated to each other, and therefore elements of both components are prerequisites for good stature estimation. Beware, however, that Fully and Pineau's statement on error rate determination is *incorrect*. The standard error of the regression line is not the 68 percent confidence interval, and twice this is not the 95 percent confidence interval (see Reporting Stature Estimates, below).

Stature Estimation From Long Bone Length

Even casual observation reveals that limb length and stature are positively associated, as are limb bone length and stature. Plots of known statures vs lengths of a long bone show that association to be linear. As a consequence, stature can be predicted from long bone lengths by simple first-order regression equations. The regression equations are derived from a database of measured long bones taken from cadavers of measured or "known" (see above) stature. Because the magnitude of the contribution of limbs and particular limb segments to stature varies somewhat predictably on the bases of sex and ancestry, separate regression equations for sex and ancestry are needed. Since large databases on which to base regression equations for many populations do not exist, one does the best one can with what is available. In many forensic situations sex is known with a higher degree of assurance than ethnicity is known, so an extensive menu of closely defined subtle ethnic choices may be less utilitarian than is often supposed. Nevertheless, it is important to pick the equation(s) that best fit the demographic description of the deceased and to have a large database sample size.

Trotter and Gleser (1952, 1958, 1977; Trotter, 1970) produced a series of regression equations based on measured cadaver height and long bone length from the Terry Collection and measured long bone length from identified World War II and Korean War casualties with known living stature. For the Terry males living stature was derived from cadaveral height by subtracting 2.5 cm. Their female sample for American blacks and whites came exclusively from the Terry Collection. For American black and white males Trotter (1970) recommended equations from World War II data. The Korean War data produced equations for "Mexican" males ($n = 112$) and "Mongoloid" males ($n = 92$). The latter group was a heterogeneous mixture of Japanese, Hawaiians, Filipinos, Amerindians, and others, which detracts from its usefulness.

A very important caution regarding the tibia length measurement for the Trotter and Gleser formulae has been presented by Jantz et al. (1995). They convincingly point out that the maximum length of the tibia measurement that Trotter and Gleser (1952) describes is, in fact, not the measurement that Trotter used to produce the Terry Collection and World War II regression equations. Contrary to the stated direction of measuring from the lateral portion of the lateral condyle to the end of the medial malleolus, the measurement should not include the malleolus, but end at the talar surface. This measurement is, in practice, much easier to take if one does not have an osteometric board with a central groove cut into the vertical wall to accommodate the intercondylar eminence. For all of the 1952 formulae the tibial measurement should extend from the lateral condyle to the talar surface and not include the malleolus. Jantz and co-workers point out that the tibial measurement(s) for the Korean War dead are uncertain and recommend that these equations not be used.

The standard operating procedure for picking the best *single* regression equation is to select the one with the smallest standard error. If the bones of the leg are present in their entirety, they are inevitably better than the bones of the arm. For the Trotter and Gleser formulae, however, the uncertainties surrounding the measurement of the tibia may detract from its use, even when regressions using that measurement may sport the smallest standard error. Therefore, if possible, the best Trotter and Gleser equations to use are in Table 7.1, along with summary data that are useful in determining confidence intervals (see below).

TABLE 7.1   Preferred Equations and Summary Data from Trotter and Gleser, 1952

	Equation	Standard Error	N	Mean	Variance
White males	2.38 fem + 61.41	±3.27	714	47.32	5.59
	2.68 fib + 71.78	±3.29	580	38.15	4.39
Black males	2.11 fem + 70.35	±3.94	80	48.24	5.04
	2.19 fib + 85.65	±4.08	68	39.80	4.92
White females	2.47 fem + 54.10	±3.72	63	42.96	6.41
	2.93 fib + 59.61	±3.57	63	34.34	4.59
Black females	2.28 fem + 59.76	±3.41	177	43.71	5.72
	2.49 fib + 70.90	±3.80	177	35.55	4.41

Genoves (1967) has offered tables and formulae for stature of a largely indigenous population from Central Mexico. Both male and female formulae are given, but the sample size is small: 22 for males and 15 for females.

For many years the conventional wisdom advocated grouping Native Americans with East Asians in most all forensic analyses. However, this may not be the best procedure. Using Fully's (1956) method to estimate living stature Sciulli and Giesen (1993) reported that, compared with East Asian populations, prehistoric Native Americans from the Ohio Valley area had relatively long legs and distal elements of the extremities. Therefore, stature estimation based on regression equations for East Asian populations will overestimate their stature. To what extent this holds true for all or most Native Americans is unknown, and there are no sets of formulae for male and female contemporary Native Americans. For the time being at least, it is probably wisest to apply Caucasian formulae.

Regression formulae for American blacks and whites, male and female, based on data submitted from modern forensic cases can be supplied by the Forensic Data Bank at the University of Tennessee, Knoxville. Sample sizes and standard errors of the regression change from time to time as new measurements are submitted, so be sure to ask for these data as well. Again, those on a PC system will want to check out FORDISC 3.

Comparison of Methods

If one compares the most widely used published methods for estimating stature from skeletal remains, it is easy to see that the Fully and Pineau regression equations (above) based on five lumbar vertebrae and either the femur or the tibia have decidedly smaller standard errors than the Trotter and Gleser equations, which are based on long bones alone. This is not surprising given the added input into the French formulations. Therefore, *so long as one is dealing with males of European descent*, it might well be advisable to use the Fully and Pineau method. However, it is important to follow the methodology correctly, including measurements and cautions.

For the Fully anatomical method (1956) there is no *regression* equation given, and, therefore, no standard error. However, in their 1960 publication Fully and Pineau do present a prediction formula

$$\text{Stature} = \text{skeletal height} + 10.8 \pm 2.05 \, \text{cm}$$

This standard error of 2.05 cm is a good proxy for the estimate of precision of the Fully anatomical method. It is decidedly smaller than any regressions based on long bones. In 1988 Lundy reported a comparison of Fully's anatomical method with Trotter and Gleser's regression equations for three military cases with recorded antemortem stature. The Fully estimate was closer to recorded stature than the Trotter–Gleser central tendency estimate in two of these cases. In one case the recorded stature lay outside the ± 1 standard error of the Trotter–Gleser estimate, but was within ± 2 standard errors.

Reporting Stature Estimates

It is hard to overstate the importance of regularly reporting 95 percent confidence intervals for stature estimates. These range from a minimum of nearly 5 inches up to more than 8 inches. In the ideal circumstance where the unknown individual is representative of an ethnic group for which there is a regression equation based on a large sample, the 95 percent confidence interval will encompass the living stature 19 out of 20 times in the long run. In other words, one can use these large intervals and still miss the stature about one in 20 times. This is if all factors, such as age corrections if appropriate, have been applied. There is no way around this 5 percent error ratio. You can do worse, but not better without increasing to, say, 99 percent confidence intervals that are far too large to have practical use. In one case I had, the reported stature for a young man was only $\frac{1}{8}$ inch inside the calculated lower 95 percent confidence limit, which drew the attention of an attorney. It happens. It also happens that stated interval and reported stature do not coincide. You may have some statistical explaining to do.

To make matters worse, 95 percent confident is often really overconfident. Perhaps the ethnicity is unknown or not represented by reliable and appropriate regression equations, an increasingly common situation as more immigrants of non-European and non-African descent, sometimes from impoverished backgrounds, join the North American population. It is a situation that requires a judgment call based on circumstances. Increasing the size of the 95 percent confidence interval by some degree to compensate for uncertainties is not out of the question.

If the long bone being used for the stature estimate is reasonably close to the mean of the sample used to produce the regression equation, then doubling the standard error interval is a decent approximation of the 95 percent confidence. However, for those one-third that are more than one standard deviation from the database mean, the 95 percent confidence interval should be calculated (see Giles and Klepinger, 1988; Klepinger and Giles, 1998 for discussion and details). The calculation for the predicted stature Y_x for bone length X is

$$Y_x \pm ts_{yx}[1 + 1/N + (X - \overline{X})^2/(N - 1)s_x^2]^{1/2}$$

where s_{yx} = sample standard error of the estimate for the regression of Y on X, X = known long bone length, $\overline{X}$ = mean of the sample database values of X, s_x^2 = variance of the sample values of X, N = sample size, and $t = t$-distribution value at the desired level (0.975) with $N - 2$ degrees of freedom.

Because the standard errors of the estimate increase as the unknown measurement or stature deviates from the sample mean, doubling the standard error to approximate the 95 percent confidence interval becomes correspondingly increasingly inaccurate.

Correcting Stature Estimates for Older Adults

> "Asked in her mid-80s how tall she was, [Babe Ruth's sister] Mamie smiled and said, 'Four feet eight, I used to be four feet ten, but I shrunk.'"
> —(Robert Creamer, "Rutholatry, or why everyone loves the Babe."
> *Smithsonian*, February 1995, pp. 68–79.)

Stature loss accompanying advancing age stems from changes and/or loss in both bone and soft tissues. Since the vertebral column is the structure responsible for the major portion of loss of standing height, stature estimates deriving from long bone measurements (wholly or in part) will overestimate stature if not corrected. Trotter and Gleser's (1951) correction, subtracting 0.06 cm for each year over 30, viewed stature loss as linearly progressive, beginning in fairly early adulthood. This assumption was challenged (Hertzog *et al.*, 1969) by a study of stature and radiogrammetric tibia length that separated male and female analyses and recognized nonlinearity of the age effect. However, the study did not offer a readily usable methodology for forensic stature estimation.

Galloway (1988) compared measured and reported statures of 550 living Caucasians aged 50–92. Her study pointed to a roughly linear loss from reported maximum stature for both men and women, probably beginning at age 45. Her recommended correction factor was to subtract from calculated stature estimates 0.16 cm for each year over 45.

In 1991 Giles utilized data from two large (over 1200 men and over 1000 women) longitudinal studies of stature change over 10 years for men and over at least 5 years for women. The longitudinal study design eliminated the confounding secular trend that affects cross-sectional studies. This study also found no stature loss before age 45. Surprisingly, the modest difference between the sexes was characterized by earlier and more pronounced stature loss among men until around age 75, when women's stature loss became permanently greater. Stature loss did accelerate with age, so a simple correction factor applicable over the 40–85 year age range is not appropriate. To abbreviate the table in Giles (1991), one can safely ignore correction before age 50. From then on the age-appropriate centimeters in Table 7.2 should be subtracted from the maximum stature calculation.

The differences between the three major methods published specifically for application to forensic stature estimation are not trivial. For example, female stature loss by age 85 calculated by the three methods gives:

Trotter and Gleser (1951)	3.3 cm (1.3 inches)
Galloway (1988)	6.4 cm (2.5 inches)
Giles (1991)	4.9 cm (1.9 inches)

Because of the sample sizes and longitudinal design, the data analyzed by Giles yield the currently best correction factors. Except for the Trotter and Gleser (1951) study using partial correlations of Terry Collection data, all of the studies rely on data from Caucasian groups only. Galloway (1988) advised that both maximum stature and age-corrected stature estimates be included in forensic reports because older people often ignore or do not recognize the extent of their height shrinkage when reporting their stature.

Age corrections are at best crude approximations. Individual pathologies, such as vertebral collapse, can result in extensive stature loss, but these can

TABLE 7.2   Centimeters to be Subtracted from Calculated Stature at Different Ages

Age	Males	Females
50	0.4	0
55	0.7	0.3
60	1.2	0.7
65	1.6	1.3
70	2.2	2.0
75	2.9	2.9
80	3.6	3.8
85	4.3	4.9

Source: from Giles (1991).

usually be readily observed and accounted for. A more subtle source of error is that estimates of age in older adults encompass very large ranges, so picking a mean age estimate for subsequently estimating stature loss is an approximation that may be off by a decade or more. In other words, anthropologists often ignore or do not recognize the extent of their uncertainty.

Secular Trend

Over the past couple of decades a great deal of discussion has centered about the forensic import of the secular trend towards increased stature in North America over the past century. For the crux of the issues see Jantz (1992, 1993), Giles (1993), Meadows and Jantz (1995), Ousley (1995), Ousley and Jantz (1998), Klepinger (2001). All of this attention may be more than the topic deserves. It is certainly true that mean stature has increased over the past century or two, but there have always been short and tall people who need to be accounted for. The 95 percent confidence interval will include their antemortem stature 95 percent of the time. The advantage of having regression formulae based on samples more representative of modern statures is that the 95 percent confidence intervals will be somewhat smaller than those for formulae based on shorter people (see Klepinger, 2001 for a discussion). The Forensic Databank comprises measurements and reported statures sent in by forensic caseworkers around the county. However, should it *necessarily* replace the Trotter and Gleser formulae? That is debatable. The Trotter and Gleser formulae also have some advantages. The formulae and statistics are published, allowing a worker to customize confidence levels, check the statistics, and even catch errors, such as the tibia measurement. They also have the advantage of using consistently measured cadaveral stature, rather than necessarily relying on many different measurers and, as we have seen, reported stature estimates of dubious accuracy. However, the Trotter and Gleser sample sizes for females could definitely be larger. Also, many of the newer immigrant groups to North America are not represented by any of the formulations. It may take some time to acquire sufficient data to produce reliable equations for the new ethnic migrants, but herein lies a really valuable potential contribution of the Forensic Database.

Stature Estimates from Fragmentary Long Bones

Situations arise in which no complete long bone can be found or accurately reconstructed. In 1970 Steele (see also Steele and Bramblett, 1988) presented regression formulae for the complete long bone from various measured long bone segments. Also included are formulae for the direct estimation of stature from fragmentary long bones when only one or both ends are missing. The equations are based on measurements from the Terry Collection for femur, tibia, and humerus. Either procedure, one regression equation or two consecutive regressions, results in standard errors that are larger than those for complete bones. The 95 percent confidence intervals are correspondingly enlarged to 8 or 10 inches. Nevertheless, such an estimate does narrow the field somewhat and may even provide an identification exclusion. For fragmentary femora Simmons *et al.* (1990) published a revised version of Steele's method. However, large standard errors persisted.

Another approach to the fragmented bone challenge has been put forth by Holland (1992), who devised regression equations for estimation of stature from measurements of the superior surface of the proximal tibia. Based on smallish sample data from the Hamann–Todd Collection, these regressions still sport hefty standard errors, but avoid the use of Trotter and Gleser tibial length equations and the problems of measurement point uncertainties associated with the Steele method.

Stature Estimation from Short Bone Length

Sometimes complete metacarpals or metatarsals may be recovered when all long bones are incomplete. Meadows and Jantz (1992) have presented regression equations based on lengths of the metacarpals. Using measurements from the Terry Collection they produced versions for male and female, black and white. All of the standard errors are about 2 inches or more, which is comparable to those based on long bone fragments, depending on the specific metacarpal and specific long bone fragment. Byers *et al.* (1989) have presented a methodology based on metatarsal length. Footwear may protect and preserve the feet when the rest of the corpse has been badly damaged.

FOOTWEAR AND FOOT LENGTH

Louise Robbins' foray into forensic interpretation of foot and shoe prints in practice and in the literature (Robbins, 1985, 1986) put this topic onto the plate of forensic anthropologists (see Chapter 11). Most would agree that standard analyses of footwear and footwear prints belongs in the criminalistics camp. However, stature estimation from foot length and shoe length can just as well fall within the purview of anthropology.

For practical forensic casework the 1991 article by Giles and Vallandigham provides the best current guidelines. Their stature prediction from foot length methods derives from a very large sample of military young men and women. As it turns out, Robbins' recommendation that a foot length/stature ratio of 15 percent be used to estimate height overestimated men's stature by an average of nearly 4 cm and underestimated women's stature by 0.8 cm. Giles and Vallandigham found that using the foot/stature ratio of 15.346 percent for men and 14.926 percent for women gave a good quick estimate of height. Variances, however, were significantly smaller if one used a regression of

height (cm) = 3.447 (foot length, cm) + 82.206 for men, and

height (cm) = 3.614 (foot length, cm) + 75.065 for women

A 70 percent confidence interval is ± 5 cm for men and ± 4.9 cm for women.

Giles and Vallandigham (1991), using data found in Robbins' article, suggest that height can be estimated from bare footprints in a hard surface using footprint length/stature ratio of 14.35 percent for men and 13.93 percent for women.

Data from the large military database were also analyzed by Gordon and Buikstra (1992), who found that stature estimates were improved if both foot length and width were included in the linear model. The same was true for professionally fitted boot dimensions. Models were slightly improved by including sex and race indicators, but these variables are rarely known in practice. The best 95 percent prediction limits for stature estimates from foot dimensions were about ± 86 mm (3.4 inch). The 95 percent intervals for boot and outsole dimensions are larger, on the order of 92 mm. Although the confidence interval numbers are larger than one would wish, they are not surprising in light of the confidence interval sizes for long bone length predictors.

Estimation of shoe size and stature from shoeprint length necessarily introduces yet another level of uncertainty, and tables and discussion can be found in the Giles and Vallandigham (1991) article. Besides the usual sources of variation in foot length, shoe size, and shoeprint length, such as shoe style and individual fitting preference, another variable has recently been thrown into the mix. According to media reports on the footwear industry, over the last few decades the plus-sizing of people has extended to their feet. Since the late 1980s the average woman's shoe has gone from size 7 to size 8 to size 9, and the percentage of women wearing size 9 has gone from 11 to 37 percent. This secular trend in bulging feet is exceeding the secular trend in stature increase (probably because body weight is a strong contributor), meaning that data collected just a couple of decades or more ago may describe a significantly smaller portion of the population. Anthropometrically, the trend for onward and upward is exceeded by onward and outward.

8

SKELETAL MARKERS OF ACTIVITY AND LIFE HISTORY

Discovering the personal identity of deceased individuals may be advanced by skeletal marks induced by certain lifestyles and life history events. Forces operating on bone, such as the pull of gravity and the pull of muscles, influence the overall mass and specific architecture or localized morphology. However, the bony oracles are often ambiguous, and interpreting their message requires cautious conservatism. For some skeletal markers the information gleaned has a high risk-to-benefit ratio. Two examples are handedness and childbirth. The benefits of correct interpretation to establishing identity are limited. The risk of incorrect information misdirecting investigators may be considerable.

Topping the list of perilous pronouncements would be estimation of body weight from the weight of dry bones. Baker and Newman's (1957) study of 125 male soldiers of the Korean war dead produced regression equations correlating skeletal weights and living weights that they interpreted as a valid estimate of normal body weight with standard errors of the estimate on the order of $\pm 13-22$ pounds. "Normal" body weight in the 1950s certainly differs from "normal" in the twenty-first century if normal is in any way defined as average. The amount of variation found in the general public is vastly greater than that of young combatants and, no doubt, is increasing as the proportion of overweight and obese people increases. Whereas the degree of muscularity can be approximated from the skeleton, the amount

Fundamentals of Forensic Anthropology, by Linda L. Klepinger of body fat cannot be. My conclusion is that in normal circumstances estimation of living weight from bone in any specific quantitative way is best left to those who wear a pointy hat with stars on it.

CHILDBIRTH INDICATORS

Erosions (depressions, scars, pits) on the dorsal surface of the pubic bones adjacent to the pubic symphyses are found very much more frequently on the pelves of females than of males. Angel (1969) was an enthusiastic advocate of the view that the pits resulted from childbirth and that the size and nature of the pits could even reflect parity. Stewart (1970) was less convinced of such a strong interpretation, but opined that there was an association with childbirth and hoped that future work with pubes from women of known parity would clarify the picture.

In 1979 two studies established the association of dorsal pits with parturition, but also revealed that the picture was not one of simple cause and affect. Kelley (1979) examined 198 pelves from the Hamann–Todd Collection for five features. The interosseous groove (associated with the interosseous ligament insertion adjacent to the L-shaped posterior superior border of the iliac auricular surface), the pre-auricular groove (sulcus), sacral pitting adjacent to the pre-auricular groove, dorsal pubic pitting, and bony lipping of the dorsal pubic margin were the five traits. The bony lipping was dropped because it appeared to be more a consequence of age than parturition, and its occurrence was not that different between parous and nulliparous women. Sacral pitting was deemed too infrequent to be of practical use. He reported that no single trait was a reliable indicator of parity. The majority of both parous and nulliparous women had no dorsal pitting; however, medium to large depressions were found in only one female designated as nulliparous. The most sensitive indicator was the pre-auricular sulcus, but it was sometimes well developed in the nulliparous. Kelley concluded that dorsal pitting, pre-auricular sulcus, and interosseous groove taken together could identify about 70 percent of pelves as parous or nulliparous, but there was no specific formulation for the decision process.

Suchey et al. (1979) reviewed pubes from 486 known-age females from 13 to 99 years of age autopsied at the Los Angeles County Department of the Chief Medical Examiner/Coroner. The number and spacing of any children were obtained from relatives or sometimes a close friend. The dorsal pits were classified in a three-way categorization: absent, trace to small, medium to large. The association between the number of full-term pregnancies and size of the dorsal scars was significant statistically, but not strongly so. The morphology of the dorsal pubis could not predict the number of births. Females who had not given birth for 15 or more years tended to larger pits than women who had given birth more recently. The inter-birth interval was not a significant factor. Seventeen reportedly nulli-parous women had medium to large dorsal pits, although it is possible that at least some of them had, indeed, given birth.

Tague (1988), looking at 352 female and 414 male pelves from prehistoric Amerindian populations and 35 known nulliparous females from the Hamann–Todd Collection, found resorption adjacent to the pubic symphysis and sacroiliac joints associated with pregnancy and parturition, but a min-ority of Amerindian females showed more severe bone resorption than that typical for males. He found no significant correlation between resorption on the dorsal pubis and in the pre-auricular area. Dorsal pitting was signifi-cantly tied to age, but resorption in the pre-auricular sulcus was not. It should be noted, however, that for the bulk of the sample, sex, age, and parity were not known, and could only be inferred.

In a review of skeletal traits purported to indicate parturition, Cox (2000) concluded that the most commonly cited traits, deep pre-auricular sulcus and dorsal pubic pitting, were not convincingly associated with obstetric history. However, she felt that the pubic tubercle extension merited more study.

All of these studies, while not in agreement about the relative value of pelvic markers for signaling childbirth, emphasize the more tenuous than hoped for relationship between birth and pelvic scarring of one sort or another. The disparate results may reflect, at least in part, the quality of the data set. The large modern collections offer known variables that prehis-toric and historic series cannot achieve. Additional variables that have not yet been investigated include the effects, if any, of nonvaginal births (Caesar-ian sections) and late-term miscarriages that would not be counted as births.

HANDEDNESS

Estimates of the prevalence of left-handedness range from about one in seven to about one in 24 (Stewart, 1979a). This range suggests either a great deal of population variation or lack of a universally accepted definition of handed-ness. For forensic purposes where establishing the handedness of the deceased usually rests on inquiries of family and friends, it is best to go with the most generally understood definition. Hence, right- and left-handedness refers to the hand used in writing, and ambidextrous refers to little preference in the hand used for writing. Degrees of ambidextrousness may vary considerably with the individual or with the specific task at hand, so to speak.

Stewart (1979a) devoted a short chapter to indicators of handedness. His discussion proposed that greater arm long bone length and beveled dorsal margin and dorsal inclination of the glenoid surface of the scapula might be indications of hand dominance on that side. His evidence, however, was tenuous and essentially anecdotal. Schulter-Ellis (1980) tested Stewart's criteria on 10 cadavers of known handedness. All but two could be diagnosed by one or more of a suite of six skeletal traits without contradiction from one of the other traits. Schulter-Ellis regarded the traits to be positive for handedness, but a sample size of 10 does not demonstrate reliable applicability to the general population.

The jugular foramina of the cranial base are often dramatically asymmetric. Moreover, one could reason that greater use of one hand would entail greater cerebral blood flow on the side controlling the dominant hand. Glassman and Bass (1986) tested the hypotheses that jugular foramen asymmetry and asymmetry in long bones of the arm were indicators of handedness. In their sample of 125 males and 57 females, all adults, they found no statistically significant chi-square values, supporting the null hypothesis of no relationship between handedness and arm bone length or jugular foramen asymmetry.

Other suggested handedness indicators have been increased arthritis and increased cortical bone thickness on the dominant side. In a blind test (Czuzak, 2005) of gross osteometric measurements, joint surface areas, mid-shaft cortical thickness, and osteoarthritis scores for arm bone and first metacarpals of 39 cadavers, Czuzak found a tendency to misclassification of handedness that was especially noted for nonright-handed individuals, females, and when using cortical thickness and joint surface areas as indicators. Czuzak suspected that the designation of handedness by next of kin did not correspond with hand usage in activities not included in the definition of handedness. This is an important point because the designated nondominant limb may be regularly involved in repetitive or strength-requiring activities.

It is my opinion that skeletal indicators of popularly defined handedness are unreliable at the present time. It is better to omit any reference to handedness in most cases because a wrong call can be very misleading. In cases where there are exceptional asymmetries, attention to handedness and other possible causes can be informative.

OTHER ACTIVITY MARKERS

Repetitive and/or strenuous activity can induce characteristic bone responses to muscular contraction and mechanical loading. Bone can respond only by loss or addition of mass, but the specific overall pattern reflects, at least to a certain extent, the nature of the stress to the skeleton. Markers of occupational stress (Kennedy, 1989) comprise a variety of skeletal signs of trauma, degeneration, robusticity, nutrition, and musculoskeletal stress markers (MSM) defined as nonpathological bone markings that occur at sites of muscle, tendon, or ligamentous attachments (Hawkey and Merbs, 1995). The markers can be either robust (hypertrophic) or erosive (hypotrophic). The robust category includes tendinous insertions and muscle to bone attachments that have a larger area of attachment. "The tendinous insertions are affected by layers of hyaline cartilage between the muscle and the bone, preventing resorption or formation of new bone, although the surrounding areas do reflect the stress of muscular pull. Stress-induced lesions have an irregular, lytic-like appearance and may be the result of continual microtrauma at the insertion site, delaying the healing process, and ultimately resulting in a necrotic appearance of remaining bone. The ossification category is due to abrupt macrotrauma, creating a bony exostosis where tissue and/or ligaments ruptured and later ossified" (Hawkey, 1998: 328–329). In forensic casework musculoskeletal stress markers attract attention only when they are out of the ordinary. A great deal of circumspection is essential in evaluating actions or movements implied by the marker pattern and translating that into a list of likely activities that could account for the pattern. Stirland (1998) cautions that quantitative and qualitative evaluations of stress lesions have poor reproducibility and that how a group of muscles works together is the clue to activity or lifestyle.

Examples of occupational stress markers found in Kennedy (1989) and Capasso et al. (1999) are instructive in the reasoning process that translates stress markers into physical activity patterns. In forensic work one may first think occupation markers, but the MSM can just as well appear on avocation enthusiasts (e.g. Saul and Saul, 1999). On the other side of the coin, sites of musculoskeletal attachments may be notable for their underdevelopment. Especially if combined with generalized or regional osteopenia (loss of skeletal mass), very gracile bones and very modest muscle markings may signal extensive bed-rest, disability, or poor mobility. This may be combined with senile osteoporosis in nursing home patients who are still able to wander off. To avoid over-interpretation of the musculoskeletal marker scores, keep in mind that, at least for the legs, MSM scores also correlate significantly with sex and especially age (Weiss, 2004).

Unlike traumatic fractures, which result from a single episode of force that exceeds the strength of bone and leads to failure, stress (or fatigue) fractures result from episodes of lesser trauma repeated over periods of weeks to months. Stress fractures are most common in young adult males and frequently result from military training (march fractures) or sports and are often on the tibia or metatarsals. Subperiosteal cortical swellings from healed stress fractures may be noticeable for several years and are not

Figure 8.1   Anterior portion of fifth lumbar vertebra with spondylolysis.

always distinguishable from healed traumatic fracture or ossified subperiosteal hematoma.

In perhaps as many as 5 percent of adult spines a lytic process between the superior and inferior articular processes of the fifth lumbar vertebra separates the lamina and spinous process from the pedicles, transverse processes and centrum (Fig. 8.1). Rarely, the fourth lumbar vertebra is involved. The condition is referred to as spondylolysis, and may be accompanied by the anterior drift of the body portion of the fifth lumbar vertebra (spondylolisthesis). The condition may or may not carry symptomatic back pain. Spondylolysis stems from localized lumbar stress consequent on vigorous physical activity. The condition is much more frequent in males than in females and suggests habitual flexion and extension of the spine (Merbs, 1996). A variety of occupational and recreational activities can provide the lytic impetus. In any event spondylolysis suggests habitual physical activity. Often in spondylolysis the posterior neural arch portion is not recovered, but the condition can be easily diagnosed from the anterior vertebral portion (Fig. 8.1).

PARTIAL MEDICAL HISTORY

Skeletal pathologies, as well as anomalies that are not in and of themselves pathological, offer insights into past and/or chronic diseases that were likely known to family and friends, and thereby might elicit identification leads.

When there is a presumptive identification of the deceased, comparison with medical records may strengthen or exclude the identity. Familiarity with the appearance of skeletal pathologies and with the nature of disease processes that produce such lesions is one of the strengths of the anthropologist well trained in skeletal biology and paleopathology. It is a strength not generally shared by physicians, most of whom have seen few, if any, macerated pathological specimens. Compendia of skeletal pathologies within a paleopathological framework are Ortner and Putschar (1985) and Aufderheide and Rodriguez-Martin (1998), and only a few of the lesions that have special relevance for forensic work will be discussed here. I have earlier reported some forensic examples (Klepinger, 1978, 1999; Klepinger and Heidingsfelder, 1996), and they will not be repeated here.

Osteoporosis of the outer table of the cranial vault was noted in some of the Korean War dead by McKern and Stewart (1957). They wondered if the condition that they noted in the remains of POWs might have been attributable to severe malnutrition over some months. However, the osteoporosis was also found among KIAs. Although McKern and Stewart did not point it out, the rates of cranial vault osteoporosis differed considerably—nine of 158 POWs and six of 292 KIAs—so the poor nutrition hypothesis is not refuted. Osteoporosis of the outer table is also found in some forensic cases (Fig. 8.2). Margaret Caldwell-Ott (personal communication) noted

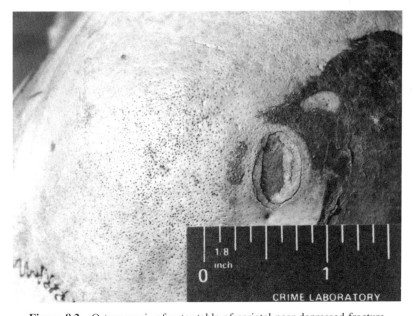

Figure 8.2   Osteoporosis of outer table of parietal near depressed fracture.

that in her experience in New York City the condition was associated with drug addiction. Of course, the chronic malnutrition that often accompanies drug addiction might be the major contributor.

Hyperostosis frontalis interna is the buildup of ridges of bone on the inner table of the frontal bone (Fig. 8.3). It has long been recognized as more common in middle-aged and older females than in other demographic segments of the population. Not all studies report similar frequencies— varying from around 13 percent to 1 percent of the general population—but the study of 1532 medico-legal autopsies by Devriendt *et al.* (2005) is in agreement with earlier studies in finding the condition very strongly associated with women over age 40. Also obesity (often of the male, apple-shaped pattern), virilism, and behavioral or psychiatric disturbances are frequently associated.

Medical Radiology

Forensic postmortem examination usually includes radiographs as standard operating procedure. When identification is an objective, radiographs can reveal pathologies and nonpathological anomalies that point to partial medical history or add anatomical data on the deceased. If there is a

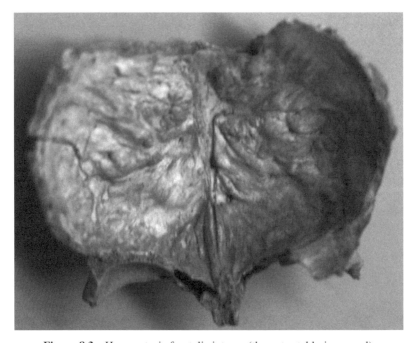

Figure 8.3   Hyperostosis frontalis interna (the outer table is normal).

presumptive identification, antemortem radiographs can be compared with postmortem radiographs of the deceased to exclude or strengthen identity (Murphy and Gantner, 1982).

Healed fractures that have occurred within the preceding decade or two—before remodeling erases the evidence radiographically and/or grossly—are useful because of their relative frequency. Location is the first item for comparison. Nonunion or poorly aligned fractures make identification easier—unless they signal lack of medical attention. Even in very well set and well-healed fractures, radiographic details of trabecular and cortical bone structure may serve to establish identity by the standard of reasonable medical certainty. To establish a positional correspondence, bone orientation on the postmortem film needs to match that of the antemortem radiographs.

In the absence of pathology, trabecular patterns as seen radiographically can strongly suggest identity, but the level of surety is much harder to estimate unless the pattern is somehow noteworthy. As in all of the criteria for establishing identity, conditions required for declaring an exclusion are more lax than those required for establishing a match.

Osteologists know that living bone's durability and apparent immutability over short time spans does not apply to durations of months to years to decades. Do skeletal changes over the course of years obliterate radiographic traits to the point of rendering them unreliable for the purposes of identification? Sauer *et al.* (1988) compared abdominal radiographs of five patients that were taken a decade or more apart. Features of the lumbar spine had not changed enough with age to thwart matching identifying traits on similarly oriented films. Although the orientation issue becomes a difficult one when the body has completely skeletonized, the lower axial skeleton remains articulated long into the body's decomposition process, so matching orientation with clinical films is feasible.

A forensic team from Seattle (Kuehn *et al.*, 2002) used medical examiner's cases to test the validity of antemortem/postmortem comparisons of chest X-rays for accuracy of decedent identification under conditions designed to mimic typical cases. The study testing one pathologist, one forensic anthropologist, and two radiologists achieved about 80 percent accuracy in correctly assigning identification or exclusion. Poor radiograph quality was the major impediment. (Sidebar: the anthropologist hit 92 percent correct; next highest was 79 percent.)

Frontal sinus patterns as seen radiographically have a long history of usefulness in establishing identification (see Ubelaker, 1984). By the standards of general acceptance in the field and precedent of acceptance in the courtroom, the essential uniqueness of individual sinus morphology for purposes of individual identification has appeared to be on solid ground, so long as the expert exercised skill and care in the antemortem/postmortem comparisons

(Kirk *et al.*, 2002). Whether or not these traditional criteria for court acceptance will hold up under *Daubert* standards is arguable. Christensen (2005) addressed such concerns in a study of 503 skull radiographs, of which 305 had simulated "antemortem" and "postmortem" duplicate shots. Elliptic Fourier analysis was used to assess the probability of correctly verifying or rejecting a putative identification, which in this study was about 96 percent. The statistical mathematics in the article requires a fair amount of sophistication, as well as significant time and resources to follow the protocol. However, Christensen concluded that the analyses strongly supported the previous assumption of individuality of frontal sinus outlines and the probable accuracy of visual assessments.

PART III

PRINCIPAL ANTHROPOLOGICAL ROLES IN MEDICAL–LEGAL INVESTIGATION

9

TRAUMA

Bone responds to traumatic impacts in ways similar to some other materials. Two phases of bone are intimately interwoven and impart two different qualities to bone tissue. The organic phase is primarily constituted of the rope-like, triple-helix protein collagen, which imparts resiliency. The inorganic phase is the calcium phosphate mineral hydroxyapatite with unit cell formula $Ca_{10}(PO_4)_6(OH)_2$, as well as amorphous calcium phosphate. There is significant substitution at both anionic and cationic positions. The inorganic phase imparts rigidity to bone tissue, but when the collagen has been greatly reduced, as in cremation, the result is brittleness. Bone that has lost significant mineral goes rubbery.

The effects that forces produce in bone vary with the proportions of organic and inorganic constituents, and this variation allows deduction about the state of the bone when the traumatic event occurred. Following death the organic phase of bone begins to decompose and lose integrity much more rapidly than the inorganic portion. Hence elasticity decreases and brittleness increases in the postmortem period.

In life, and for a period of time after death that varies with the environmental conditions, the relatively high collagen content results in more plastic response to bending or impact than is seen in bone that has undergone organic loss. In the latter case dead bone is similar to dead wood: it snaps rather cleanly. In contrast, living or recently living bone behaves as green wood when bent or hit; often there is longitudinal splitting and an arc peels away just as when one attempts to snap an unseasoned branch. The greenstick fracture is evidence that the force was applied at or around the time of death, that is, was *perimortem.* Sharp breaks without any evident curvature are more suggestive of *postmortem* impact. *Antemortem*, or premortem, injury is indicated if the wound shows *any* evidence of healing. Evidence of healing on the skeleton requires an absolute minimum of a week (Sauer, 1998). Another sign of antemortem or perimortem fracture is the presence of adherent bone fragments (Ortner and Putschar, 1985). Small fragments of fractured bone may adhere to adjacent bone *only if* periosteum is intact at the time the fracture was produced. Zuo and Zhu (1991) have been able to use scanning electron microscopy to analyze fibrin networks at fracture sites that are only found in antemortem bone fractures, and that may distinguish perimortem from postmortem injury.

BLUNT FORCE TRAUMA

Frying pans, rolling pins, fists, feet, pipes, and ball bats are but a tiny fraction of potential weapons that can inflict blunt trauma. Galloway's (1999) edited book on blunt force trauma should be consulted for coverage of skeletal damage that is both detailed and inclusive. Another excellent article with illustration is Berryman and Symes (1998).

Cranial Fracture

Blunt trauma to the cranial vault can produce localized depressed fractures that when shallow may heal over to resemble a thumbprint dent in clay. More powerful blows may push the inner table into the cranial space (Fig. 9.1). Sometimes an impression of the weapon is left in the skull. In the case of a powerful blow to the head, the aforementioned elastic property of bone comes into play. Inbending at the site of impact triggers compensatory outbending at some radial distance from the impact. Viewed from outside the skull the central impact is in compression, and the peripheral upheaving is in tension. Since bone is weaker in tension than in compression, initial fracturing may occur in the area of outbending some distance from the point of impact. The fracture can then propagate along the line or lines of least resistance as the energy of impact travels along the line(s). Besides lines of tension, other paths of least resistance for fracture propagation are areas of gradual curvature, as opposed to areas of sharp curvature, and along suture lines. In skulls with open sutures the energy can dissipate along the sutures without leaving any observable fracture line. When sutures are partly or wholly united they remain areas of natural weakness, but a fracture line along the sutural path is noticeable (Fig. 9.2).

(a)

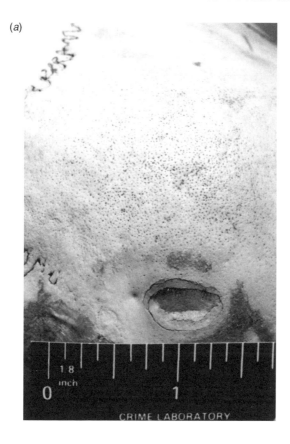

(b)

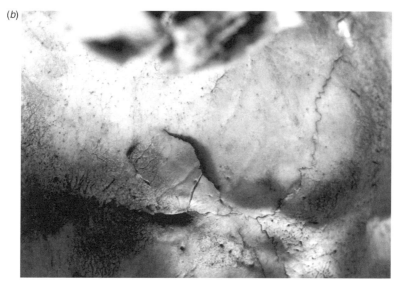

Figure 9.1   (a) Depressed focal cranial fracture, external view. (b) Interior view of depressed fracture in (a) with inner table encroaching on intracranial space.

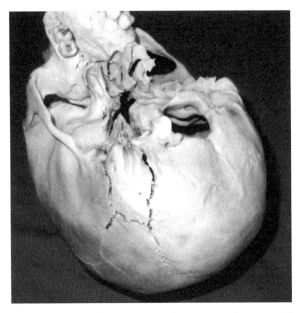

Figure 9.2   Fracture line following suture lines surrounding mastoid temporal.

Just as nonunited sutures dissipate the energy imparted by a blow, so do pre-existing fracture lines. In this case bone acts as a material in ways that are reminiscent of the fracture response of glass and concrete: a fracture track from a second blow will not cross a preexisting fracture. A subsequent fracture will end at the T-like intersection with a pre-existing fracture as its energy is propagated along the earlier fracture.

Prior to fracture, the bending of cranial bone in response to trauma may exceed the elastic limit of bone and can cause permanent deformation. This deformation can make accurate reconstruction of the pre-impact skull impossible because the deformed bone shards do not return to their original dimensions (Fig. 9.3). However, the deformation itself can serve as evidence. Because elasticity is a property of the collagen phase, its presence, as recorded in the deformation, points to perimortem injury. It is, in effect, a greenstick fracture. Moreover, the deformations frozen into the bone can help reconstruct the point(s) of impact.

When repeated strong blows are struck to same area of the cranium, the edges of already fractured bone rub against one another and frequently cause spalling or flaking along the margins. The mechanism and appearance of the chipping recall the mechanism and product of pressure flaking in flint knapping.

Facial fractures commonly present as healed, as well as perimortem. Fractures around the nose, nasals, and/or maxillae are the common result of blows to the face. The high frequency of nasal fractures in modern

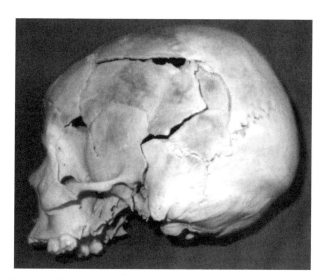

Figure 9.3   An area of the parietal adjacent to a depressed semicircle is permanently out-wardly deformed. Areas of bone flaking along the shard margins, along with bending and fracture patterns, strongly suggest more than one blow to the left side of the skull.

Americans appears to result from interpersonal violence, notwithstanding some attributable to accident and sports injury (Walker, 1997).

Hyoid Fracture

The hyoid bone lying high in the throat area is sheltered from many of the blows of accidental and even inflicted trauma. A fractured hyoid triggers special attention by pathologists and anthropologists because of its associ-ation with manual strangulation. However, this association is far from being indicative of the occurrence or nonoccurrence of manual strangulation. Several additional considerations must come into play. O'Halloran and Lundy (1987) pointed out the importance of the presence or absence of bony fusion to likelihood of fracture. In youth the greater horns (cornua) are connected to the body via cartilage. There is a trend towards bony union of the cornua to the body with increasing age. In spite of this trend, the feature is too variable to provide a reliable criterion for age estimation. Nevertheless, fusion is more common in the elderly than in younger aged individuals. Flexibility of the hyoid segments united only by cartilage is sig-nificantly greater than the fused hyoid, so it can absorb considerable more pressure without breaking. The frequency of hyoid fracture in children is neg-ligibly small. Fusion of the horns to the body in adulthood may be unilateral or bilateral. In the unilateral situation a certain amount of flexibility is retained in the stressed bone, and unilateral fusion is more common in women than in men, occuring in about one-third of adult women (O'Halloran and

Lundy, 1987). Unfractured hyoid does not eliminate strangulation as a cause of death.

Ubelaker (1992) reviewed the literature and presented some guidelines on hyoid fracture. Although there was great variation in reports of hyoid fracture with hanging, averaging all cases, about 8 percent of hyoids were fractured. Eleven percent of ligature strangulations caused hyoid fracture, as did 34 percent of manual strangulations. Pollanen and Chiasson (1996) looked at a small sample of ligature and manual strangulation and found bony fusion in 70 percent of fractured hyoids, but only 30 percent of unfractured hyoids. They also found that hyoid shape differed between the fractured and unfractured.

Fracture of the thyroid and cricoid cartilages can also occur in hangings and strangulations, but these do not ossify until the later years, and so are of limited usefulness with skeletonized remains. Demonstrating perimortem fracture in this situation requires very careful examination, and still may not be definitive.

Postcranial Fracture

Galloway (1999a) and Whiting and Zernicke (1998) devote considerable detailed description and illustration to the biomechanics, classification, and analysis of bone fracture. Very broadly, complete fracture of a long bone can be morphologically classified as transverse, oblique, spiral, comminuted (shattered), butterfly (triangular wedge of bone), and segmental. Each type is characteristically produced by one or a combination of applied forces: compression, tension, rotation, shear, and bending. Fracture patterns are also subject to modification depending on the size of the instrument, the magnitude of the force, and the area onto which it is applied. For instance, focal (or tapping) force often produces a transverse fracture, and a large force over a large area (crushing) is likely to produce a wedge-shape fracture. A car bumper hitting a pedestrian can cause the latter. The focal force typically breaks only one of two paired bones in the forearm and lower leg. The defensive, "parry" fracture of the ulna shaft incurred in attempts to ward off blows to the head or face is a classic example.

CHILD ABUSE

The editors' note to the fourth edition of *The Battered Child* (Helfer and Kempe, 1987) comments on the life of C. Henry Kempe. "Since he first coined the phrase 'the battered child syndrome' twenty-five years ago, over fifty thousand children have been killed by the very parents charged with their safety and at least twenty-five million more have been abused, neglected, or sexually exploited" (p. xi). This sad statistic implies likelihood that the forensic anthropologist will become involved in such cases. Child murder and physical child abuse can involve skeletal as well as soft tissue injuries. When injuries to a living or dead child are brought to light, the caretaker (usually a parent or other household member) typically attributes them to accidental causes. In the absence of any eyewitnesses to a purported fall or vehicular injury the clinician or death investigator needs to assess the plausibility of accidental vs intentionally inflicted trauma.

The anthropologist may be recruited to help assess evidence of skeletal injury, usually, but not exclusively, when skeletonized or highly decomposed remains are found. The anthropologist's contribution stems from a deep familiarity with skeletal tissue that is often not shared by the physician. Bioarchaeology, and especially paleopathology, inform the assessment of skeletal injury. As Walker *et al.* (1997) point out, direct examination of the skeleton or macerate by experienced physical anthropologists can reveal healed trauma after the lesion has become radiologically invisible. Included here are old well-healed fractures and ossified subperiosteal hematomas (bone bruises) that have resolved to the point of radiological invisibility. Kerley (1976, 1978) was one of the first to employ extensive knowledge of osseous paleopathology to the recognition and analysis of battered-child skeletons, and similar efforts continue (e.g. Galloway, 1999b).

The pre-school-age child is statistically the most vulnerable to abuse, so most clinical and pathological studies focus on infants and young children (Leventhal *et al.*, 1993). Radiological surveys indicate skeletal trauma to be most frequent in the extremities, the skull, and the rib cage—in that order (Di Maio and Di Maio, 1993). The hallmark of chronic child abuse is multiple fractures in various stages of healing (Kerley, 1978). Single-incident battery is less obvious, but certain patterns of fracture are highly suspicious, especially in infants who have little opportunity for misadventure.

Some consider metaphyseal and rib fractures in infants to be diagnostic of abuse (Kleinman *et al.*, 1995; Di Maio and Di Maio, 1993). Barsness *et al.* (2003) looked further into the close correlation of rib fractures with non-accidental trauma. They found that, in children under 3 years, the positive predictive value of rib fractures was 95 percent or greater, depending on the history and clinical circumstances. (The positive predictive value is the answer to the question, given the presence of rib fracture, what is the probability of intentional injury?) Moreover, the study found rib fracture(s) to be the only skeletal manifestation of intentional trauma in 29 percent of children.

Skull fracture, although less frequent than long bone fracture, is responsible for more death and lasting injury. Explanations such as a fall from a bed or sofa are suspect. Helfer *et al.* (1977) reviewed 85 hospital incidents where children under the age of 5 fell from beds, cribs, or examination tables. Such falls are typically from about 36 inches and almost always to a noncarpeted floor. In 57 of the 85 incidents there was no apparent injury; in 17 there were small cuts and/or bloody noses; 20 children had a bump or bruise; one child had a small unilateral skull fracture without any signs of intracranial injury. They concluded that claims of serious head injury from a child falling from a bed or sofa should be regarded as suspicious. Williams (1991) concluded from his study that infants and small children free-falling from less than 10 feet are unlikely to be seriously or fatally injured. Meservy *et al.* (1987) found that multiple fractures, bilateral fractures, and fractures crossing sutures occurred significantly more frequently in documented abuse cases than in accidental trauma. Another clinical study of 89 children under 2 years of age (29 of the children with definite nonaccidental injury) found that skull fractures in abused children were more frequently depressed, wide, and measuring more than half a centimeter. They involved more than one cranial bone, involved nonparietal fracture, and had associated intracranial injury including subdural hematoma (Hobbs, 1984).

Chronically abused children may display localized areas of subperiosteal new bone formation, especially on the bones of the arms and legs. The new bone formation is the ossification of subperiosteal hematomas that are caused by traumatic stripping of the periosteum away from the underlying bone and concomitant rupture of the blood vessels. Such "bone bruises" can follow flogging of the arms, legs, or head, or yanking or twisting an arm or leg. In infants the periosteum is rather loosely attached and easily separated from the bone. The frequency of subperiosteal hematomas is probably underestimated in radiographic surveys of living children because the ossified state looks much like normal bone.

Chronic neglect has skeletal manifestations, but they are more subtle and less specific than episodic trauma. Failure to thrive, very small size for age, episodic stress indicators such as growth arrest lines in teeth and bones, poor dental health with absent or deficient dental care are all suggestive of parental negligence (Walker *et al.*, 1997). However, these indicators by themselves are usually insufficient to be actionable, but they may serve as important corroborative evidence in building a case for protection or prosecution.

Kerley (1976, 1978; see also Crist *et al.*, 1997) has cautioned against overinterpreting skeletal lesions. For example, clefts in the occipital bone may result from developmental irregularities unrelated to abuse; yet to the inexperienced eye they may appear to be bone fractures. Crist *et al.* (1997) stress that postmortem cranial bone displacement in the immature neurocranium can be misinterpreted as evidence of antemortem cranial trauma. Because the sutures do not begin to fuse before adolescence, trauma to the head in children often results in separation along the suture line rather than bone fracture. Taphonomic forces, such as sunlight or variations in temperature and humidity can also cause bone displacement along suture lines. The essential difference between the two causes is that premortem blunt trauma will depress the impacted bone inward with respect to its surrounding bones, and in postmortem bone displacement the affected bone is raised outward from its surrounding bones.

Multiple and frequent fractures in young children may also be caused by some diseases, such as osteogenesis imperfecta. Likewise, there may be disease (e.g. hemophilia) causality for subperiosteal hematoma, or nutritional causes such a vitamin C deficiency. Albeit, the latter might require some explanation as to why neglect might not be a factor. Hypervitaminosis-A can produce symmetrical rib fractures. Parents can be wrongly accused of intentional child injury as a consequence of their own or somebody else's ignorance about parenting practices, dietary requirements, or the correct medical history. The main point is that skeletal evidence seen in a vacuum cannot make the case for child abuse or neglect, but it can furnish important biological data to support or rebut the picture drawn from medical and behavioral data.

Finally, there is the surprisingly frequent phenomenon of mummified neonate remains. These may retain the umbilical cord. Typically the remains are wrapped in blankets or towels, placed in trunks or other containers, and may be several decades old. Efforts to identify the infants and to ascertain stillbirth, live birth, and cause of death are often futile.

PENETRATING AND PERFORATING TRAUMA

Injury from penetrating and perforating trauma can result from a variety of accidental circumstances, as well as from hostile encounters with members of the Knife and Gun Club. Penetrating wounds are those that enter the body, but do not exit. Perforating wounds are through-and-through.

Gunshot Wounds

Gunshot wound is essentially a category of blunt trauma caused by a very powerful force acting on a small focal area (Di Maio and Di Maio, 1993), so many of the reactions of bone tissue to gunshot will follow the same material principles as mentioned above. However, there is a substantial variation in the effect on bone depending on such factors as power of the firearm (hence bullet velocity), size of the bullet, construction of the bullet, and range of fire. Therefore, volumes can be and have been written. This section will present only some of the more commonly encountered gunshot wounds. An excellent discussion of the mechanics of gunshot wounds is found in Berryman and Symes (1998) and Whiting and Zernicke (1998).

The cranial puncture wound caused by a pointed object or bullet produces (on the impact side) a well-defined hole, which is usually not the case in postmortem erosion. The wound is larger on the internal surface of the hole than on the external surface. This internal beveling is produced by shards of bone knocked free from the internal surface. Analogous cases are the conical chips thrown by a stone hitting a windshield and bulbs of percussion produced in flint knapping. In other words, the entry side is sharp edged, and the exit side shows a larger, inward-sloped bevel (Figs 9.4 and 9.5). In the case of a through-and-through wound a second external bevel on the ectocranial surface of the exit site may also form (Rhine and Curran, 1990). The bevel on the side opposite the impact surface is attributable to the fact that the table of compact bone away from the surface of impact is under tensile stress, while the table of the impact surface is under compressive stress. As mentioned before, bone is weaker under tensile stress than under compressive stress, producing the wider fracture pattern on the tensile side. (The same phenomenon is responsible for producing the "butterfly" pattern in a leg bone.) Beveling of wounds in bone can be very useful in tracking a bullet's direction of travel. Areas of thin bone, such as the squamous temporal, will not display the bevel pattern.

The fracture pattern of ballistic impact to the cranium often follows the same sequence as that resulting from severe blunt trauma. Typically, bullets entering the cranial vault produce radial fractures emanating from the primary entry hole. As the bullet travels through the brain, it slows and gives up energy to the surrounding brain, which has roughly the consistency of Jell-O. The transferred energy increases intracranial pressure, which may, in turn, result in concentric heaving fractures. Concentric ectocranially directed heaving fractures develop perpendicular to the radiating fractures. Sometimes one generation of circumferential hoop fractures is not sufficient to disperse the intracranial pressure, and another generation of peripheral concentric heaving fractures occurs. Absence of secondary radiating fractures suggests either low-energy bullets or that the generated intracranial pressure was dissipated along patent suture lines or pre-existing fractures. Fractures initiated at the entry site propagate through the cranial bone faster than the bullet passes through to the opposite side. A newly propagating fracture will not cross a pre-existing fracture. Radial fractures may occur alone when they are sufficient to relieve generated pressure, but concentric heaving fractures are never seen without radial fractures. The projectile

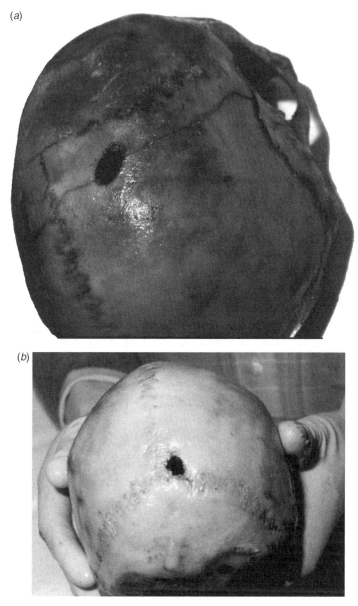

Figure 9.4   (*a*) The first gunshot wound to the head produced radial fractures. (*b*) The second to the same head did not produce radial fractures.

loses energy as it travels through the cranium and may not have the energy to exit the skull at all. When it does, radial fractures are not as long and often terminate in pre-existing fractures, and any concentric heaving fractures are smaller in diameter than those on the entry side. These relationships

Figure 9.5 Exit side (cerebral surface) of twin gunshot wounds showing bevels.

are crucial in establishing trajectories and sequence of fire in multiple wounds.

However, this summary of principles of skeletal effects of ballistics disguises the tremendous variation attributable to velocity and bullet characteristics such as diameter (caliber), fragmentation, design, and deformation. The kinetic energy of ballistic impact is directly proportional to the mass of the bullet and to the square of its velocity. Velocity has a much greater contribution to a bullet's destructive energy. Doubling the mass of the bullet will double its kinetic energy, but doubling its velocity will boost its energy by a factor of 4. A very high-velocity bullet may blow the skull apart.

It seems reasonable that the size of the wound diameter should be determined by the size of the bullet. However, Berryman *et al.* (1995) warn workers that caution is paramount in estimating caliber from wound diameter. Yes, .38 caliber bullets produce significantly bigger wounds than .22 or .25 caliber, but wound size from the latter two cannot be distinguished. Moreover, acute angle and tangential shots can produce very irregular patterns, such as the "keyhole" wound, shaped like its namesake—that is, a keyhole for a skeleton key (Dixon, 1982). The circular entrance wound with internal bevel is continuous with a triangular site with external bevel that marks the exit of formed bone fragments (Fig. 9.6). Some holes may be larger than the caliber, and, in rare circumstances, smaller than the caliber. A bullet just grazing the skull can create a gutter wound

Figure 9.6   Outer table entrance side of keyhole gunshot wound.

(Di Maio, 1985). Bullets can follow bizarre tracks. Entrance and exit wounds occasionally masquerade as one another and as blunt trauma. Each case requires careful consideration on its own terms.

The nature of shotgun wounds may vary widely depending on gauge of the shotgun and firing distance. Because shot is small and travels at lower velocity, it is more likely to imbed in the skeleton. Radiographic imaging of the skeleton can help detect the pattern and spread of injury. The kinetic energy of 12 gauge blasts is half as great again as for 20 or .410 gage, and a greater volume of gas is produced, making contact wounds far more devastating—12 gauge is much more likely to burst the head and blow out the brain (Harruff, 1995). The effects of 16 gauge shotguns are somewhere in the middle (Harruff, 1995). This order is consonant with the degree of recoil for the gauges.

Gunshot wounds to the postcranium may vary somewhat from the guidelines presented above; they often do not make the clearly identifiable holes seen in the skull. For instance, low-velocity bullets typical of small caliber handguns usually cause moderate-grade comminuted (splintered) fractures of a femoral diaphysis; the high-velocity rounds more typical of rifles produce more extensive fracture damage (Whiting and Zernicke, 1998). Like high-power rifles, close-range shotgun wounds can also cause severe damage to the soft tissue. When bullets hit ribs or vertebrae, they often cause fracture damage that is hard to distinguish from other forms of focused blunt trauma (Fig. 9.7). Sometimes recovered clothing reveals hole(s) typical of bullets, or a careful search of the area turns up bullets, helping to pinpoint the true source of the trauma and/or cause of death. Gunshot wounds in flat portions of postcranial bones resemble cranial wounds with well-defined entrance side and beveled or deformed exit side

Figure 9.7   Gunshot wound to rib resembling focal blunt trauma.

(Fig. 9.8). Beware the circular defect left from the imperfect fusion of the segments of the youthful sternal body. These defects are not so uncommon and can look very much like a bullet hole to the chest, except that the margins are smooth and unbroken.

Sharp Injuries

Incised wounds (cuts, incisions) are longer than they are deep, in contrast to stab wounds that are deeper than they are wide. The distinction may not always be clear when one is dealing with skeletal material. Stab wounds can result either from thrusting or from the victim falling on something sharp or pointed. Absence of sharp instrument stigmata on the skeleton does not mean that sharp injury was not the cause of death; many fatal wounds miss the skeleton altogether. Except for guns, knives are probably the most frequently used weapons in homicides, but the average household contains many other potential spears and blades. Knife blades typically leave a V-shaped cut in the bone. A single thrust may produce two noncontiguous bone wounds, for instance, one on the inferior aspect of a rib and another on the superior aspect of the rib just below it. In such a circumstance a double-edged blade wound tends to leave two V-shaped cuts. A single-edged blade might leave a V-shaped cut and a nearby squared off wound caused by the blunt trauma of impact from the back of the blade (Maples, 1986). A blade going into fresh bone compresses the bone on both sides of the V, but when the blade is withdrawn, the bone will tend to rebound to the extent that the width of the bone cut may be less than the width of the blade that created it (Maples, 1986). Sometimes a stab wound track can be

(a)

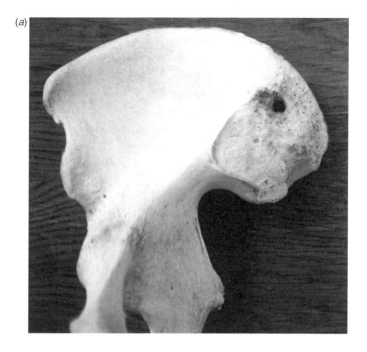

(b)

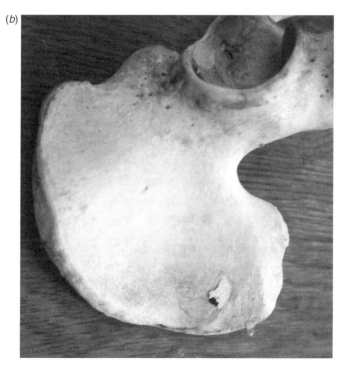

Figure 9.8   (*a*) Entrance side view, and (*b*) exit side view of gunshot wound to ilium.

longer than the blade itself because a strong blow can compress the body wall, even the chest wall. Thus, it may be possible to partially describe a weapon from the bone damage, but only with much care. Often the knife wounds in bone are simply nicks that are easy to overlook without careful inspection of the remains. Perimortem knife wounds can raise or curl an edge of an incision in classic greenstick fashion noticeable on the gross specimen. In some cases scanning electron microscopy can indicate directionality of a slashing cut, whether the cut was made on fresh or dried bone, and match a specific instrument to its specific mark (Houck, 1998), but this is highly specialized work.

Just as the lack of sharp trauma evidence does not exempt knives from the possible weapons list, the converse is also true: presence of incised marks on bones does not translate to a knife as a murder weapon. Attempts to disarticulate a corpse can leave cut marks about the joints of the extremities and on the cervical vertebrae. Coincidentally, these same areas are favorites of larger scavengers, but tooth marks and knife marks are can be differentiated most of the time, given sufficient experience on the part of the observer. It is a good idea to make a few sample cuts on bone with an autopsy saw and learn to recognize such marks so that autopsy artifacts will not be confused with perpetrator-induced phenomena. Finally, some farm machinery inadvertently running over a corpse can simultaneously mimic and camouflage cut marks.

10

THE POSTMORTEM PERIOD

ESTIMATION OF THE POSTMORTEM INTERVAL

In act V, scene I, Hamlet asks, "How long will a man lie i' the earth ere he rot?" The non-Shakespearean inelegant answer is "it depends . . ." The longer the elapsed time since death the more imprecise are the chronological indicators and the broader the estimated time period. The broader the estimated time period since death, the more frustrated or exasperated are the death investigators. Extended elapsed time periods are the purview of the anthropologist. The earlier stages of decomposition are usually best evaluated by forensic pathologists and forensic entomologists, but will be briefly reviewed here. More extensive coverage can be found in books on forensic medicine and in Gill-King (1997) and Micozzi (1991).

Upon death the body temperature begins to drop. The rate of postmortem drop in body temperature, *algor mortis*, is influenced by ambient temperature, clothing, or covering, position of the body, degree of fatness, and body temperature at the time of death. *Rigor mortis* is stiffening of the body that begins at death and usually becomes noticeable after 2–4 h. Rigor results from the loss of adenosine triphosphate (ATP) from muscles, and at room temperature this tends to peak within 12 h and disappear by 24–48 h following death. Rapid cooling of the body, as by refrigeration, will delay the onset and disappearance. Exertion, high fever, and convulsions

Fundamentals of Forensic Anthropology, by Linda L. Klepinger
Copyright © 2006 John Wiley & Sons, Inc.

accelerate the onset. Rigor usually begins in the small muscles of the head and relaxes first in that area. The elderly and infants, who have little muscle mass, exhibit poorly developed rigor. *Livor mortis* is the purplish discoloration of the skin in areas of gravitational pooling of blood after circulation has stopped. Onset times are about the same as for rigor—manifested in 2–4 h and "fixed", or permanent, in 8–12 h. If the body position is moved before that time, there may be primary and new areas of livor.

Other commonly employed guides for the postmortem time period of hours to a few days include the increase in potassium in the vitreous humor of the eye, degree of digestion of stomach contents, and skin slippage. Skin slippage with loss of hair and nails and shedding of the skin of the hands and feet in a glove and stocking fashion usually occurs within about 4–7 days.

Forensic anthropologists are sometimes involved when the postmortem period is only a week or two, but are more frequently called upon when the interval is on the order of months to years. An extensive literature, including two books on forensic taphonomy edited by Haglund and Sorg (1997, 2002a), discusses the interpretation of clues about the course of events undergone by the body from the time of death until recovery.

Degradation begins immediately after death. Breakdown of body tissues by internal enzymes is termed *autolysis*. Internal microorganisms proceed with anaerobic decomposition of tissues—the foul-smelling *putrefaction*. As these microbes tear down tissue they create gases which are initially trapped under the skin and cause bloating. Bloating is especially prominent in the regions of the abdomen and face. The skin discolors, blisters, and peels. The progress of decay has been variously divided into about four to six arbitrary stages, five perhaps being the most common: fresh, bloat, active decay, advanced (rancid) decay, and dry remains. Much of process and timing of decomposition in eastern Tennessee and environmentally similar areas has been investigated at the Anthropological Research Facility at the University of Tennessee, Knoxville. Not surprisingly, sheltering the corpse from insects and scavengers and high temperatures slows decay. Other things being equal, decay is slower for buried corpses than for surface remains and slower with deep burial than with shallow burial (Rodriguez and Bass, 1985; Mann *et al.*, 1990; Bass, 1997). Vass *et al.* (1992) used ratios of volatile fatty acids in soil solution and accumulated degree-days to estimate time since death.

Consistency of tissue is an important determinant of the sequence of degradation. The brain is first to degrade and the bones and teeth are last. More superficial fatty tissues can become resistant to decomposition by forming adipocere, a.k.a. gravewax, a peculiar waxy substance resulting from the saponification of fatty acids. Adipocere formation is characteristic of moist postmortem conditions and submersion. Adipocere may persist for a very long time, sometimes for decades and even on the order of centuries (Pfeiffer *et al.*, 1998), but has not yet served as a good postmortem clock. The quantity of adipocere produced can be massive in the case of obese corpses.

Postmortem pink teeth were at one time thought to be possible indicators of strangulation or suffocation. The pink teeth are caused by the autolysis of erythrocytes that free hemoglobin into the tubules of the dentine. The hemoglobin-packed dentin viewed through the enamel of the crown appears pink; the enamel-free roots may appear even redder. Because the young have comparatively large pulp chambers and more vasculature, they display pink teeth more readily than adults do. Postmortem pink teeth are most commonly associated with decomposition in wet environments, but can also result from heating or freezing (Kirkham *et al.*, 1977).

If the body is accessible, the five major stages of decay are accompanied by serial successional waves of carrion insects and other arthropods. A particular stage of succession can, given a modicum of environmental information—especially temperature—help to estimate the time since death. Estimation of the postmortem interval (PMI) is the most frequently employed aspect of forensic entomology. Several guides are available on forensic entomology; two possible starting places for the nonspecialist are Catts and Haskell (1990) and Haskell *et al.* (1997).

The first blow flies may arrive to lay eggs within a few hours, or in some cases within an hour of death. The fly larvae, that is, maggots, feed on the corpse and go through a series of developmental stages before pupating. Different species of flies arrive at different stages of decomposition. Some arthropods prefer dry remains and even skeletonized remains. Not all of these visitors to the body are strict carrion eaters; some are predators on other insects. The time frame for the succession is dependent on environmental conditions and other factors not infrequently associated with discovered bodies. Even when bodies are discovered during the winter, the presence of insect remains or pupae indicate that the remains were in a certain putrefactive stage during the period when these species were active. Bugs on drugs—that is, carrion eaters consuming heroine containing tissue—develop faster than usual and can falsely inflate the PMI estimate (Goff *et al.*, 1991). However, heroine can be detected in the insect tissue, providing information about the deceased as well as about the PMI. The natural body orifices are usually the first areas of the body to receive insect attention. Areas of injury and broken skin attract ovipositing blowflies and can also serve as portals for bacteria. Consequently, such areas are degraded faster than would otherwise be the case, and localized maggot masses suggest looking for injury in that area.

The odor of decomposition may be present for months or years after the soft tissues have disappeared. The inside of the skull is a good place to detect any residual odor. Soaking of bones may also bring out faint odor. Detection of odor suggests a PMI of a few years, certainly less than 10. Hair masses and fragments of periosteum attached to the bone may remain for months or even years.

All aspects of the nature and rate of decomposition are dependent upon the immediate environment. High altitude and arctic conditions can preserve soft tissue for a very long time. The process and timing of decay in the arid southwestern United States (Galloway, 1997) can be very different from the Tennessee standards. Dry conditions can dehydrate all or part of a body before the agents of decay and arthropod feasting have disposed of the soft tissue, resulting in complete or partial mummification. Caves and high altitude, as well as deserts, frequently foster mummification. Partial mummification can also be found in more humid regions, especially when bodies have been heavily clothed or wrapped in blankets, sleeping bags, carpets, and the like (see Fig. 10.1).

A variety of environmental conditions affect the degree of preservation or decay of the skeleton. Archaeologists are familiar with many of them: acidity of the soil, exposure to weathering, and depth of burial. Burial beneath the water table or above, graves shallow enough to be subject to repeated freezing and thawing, and placement in one or another root zone can all depend on depth. Roots usually follow vascular channels, and it usually takes several years for them to infiltrate significantly—on the order of two to three decades if the burial was in a shallow root zone. Bone fragments on the surface, say from an airplane crash, may sometimes be penetrated by roots after less than 10 years, and deeply buried bones may never be penetrated by roots at all (Kerley, 1973). Surface finds can show great variation in preservation from one microenvironment to another. Portions of the skeleton exposed to direct sunlight dry out more quickly, bleach, and may eventually exfoliate on the exposed surface. The drying and bleaching can happen in a matter of a few months, even in temperate latitudes. When parts of the same body have been exposed to sunlight while others have been shaded, the shaded portions appear to be much more recent.

A large body of literature on the decomposition and transport of submerged bodies is fairly recent. Haglund and Sorg (2002b) offer a good review of this topic, and that would be a good place to start.

As the PMI stretches into decades it becomes increasingly hard to distinguish a potential "cold case" from historic or archaeological remains, especially if there are no associated artifacts. An excellent indicator, if available for examination, is dental attrition. Modern diets in developed countries have lost almost all of the grit introduced by stone grinding and hastily gathered molluscs. As a result tooth wear is minimal compared with earlier times. Even in the nineteenth century, dental wear was noticeably more pronounced

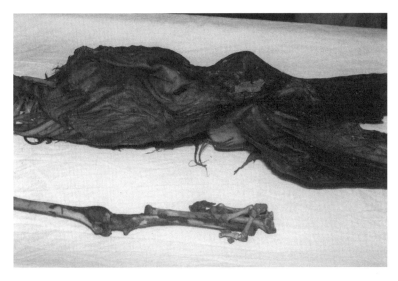

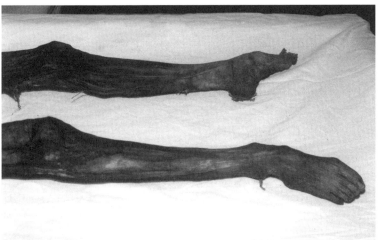

Figure 10.1 Partial mummification of body wrapped in a sleeping bag in a humid climate.

than today, but not so great as in prehistoric populations (Fig. 10.2). For many archaeological groups even newly erupted dentition can betray a greater attrition rate by the differences among the first, second and third molars (Fig. 10.3). Even a single worn tooth may point to a case no longer of forensic concern. Dental restorations can be indicative of modern or historical time frames (although the two differ), but the converse is not true. Lack of any evidence of professional dental care is fairly common in recent remains. Lacking cultural or dental evidence, one is on much less solid ground in estimating elapsed time since death. Even experienced anthropologists have been fooled. Preservation is perfidious.

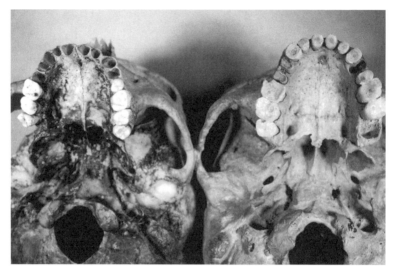

Figure 10.2   Modern forensic skull on the left compared with an archaeological skull on the right, showing difference in dental attrition.

POSTMORTEM EVENTS

A corpse may be subject to innumerable kinds of treatments, and sorting out this taphonomy may offer important information about the deceased individual, the circumstances surrounding the death, and facts about a perpetrator.

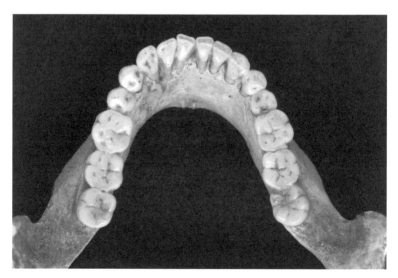

Figure 10.3   Mandible of archaeological origin with recently erupted third molars and wear already apparent on the first and second molars.

"Taphonomy concerns the comprehension of multiple factors which play a role in the disintegration and scatter of a body and its accoutrements until they have been environmentally recycled and incorporated into the earth, its waters, its air, and its inhabitants" (Davis, 1997: xv). This section introduces those taphonomic events that are most frequently encountered in forensic practice, although it should be remembered that the impetus for studying taphonomy originated with archaeology.

Carnivore Scavenging

The inventory of carrion scavengers varies considerably with the environment. In nonwater contexts the "large" carnivores will always include dogs and cats and often raccoons along with regional fauna. Smaller carnivores include some birds and a variety of rodent species. Hallmarks of large animal activity include jagged chewed ends of long bones and ribs, puncture wounds compatible with canine teeth, and sometimes—with very large carnivores—spiral fractures. Blumenschine *et al.* (1996) defined four types of bone scarring produced by carnivores. Punctures result from canines piercing the bone. Pits result when the bone is compressed but not pierced. Scores are scratches to the bone surfaces from gnawing, usually along the contours; rodent gnawing produces parallel scoring grooves that can sometimes be extensive. Furrows are longitudinal gash marks resulting from attempts to access the marrow. Rodents and cattle may chew old, essentially dry, bones—rodents apparently for wearing down incisors and both rodents and herbivores for acquiring needed dietary minerals.

Animal scavenging is far more common when bodies are accessible through doors and windows, exposed on the ground surface, or very shallowly covered. Haglund *et al.* (1989; Haglund, 1997) looked at the sequence of events from canid activity. Although the study was based in the Pacific Northwest, the sequence probably fairly represents the course of events in other environments. The initial stage involves removal of soft tissue only without any body disarticulation. The first skeletal damage is typically to the ventral chest, along with removal of upper limbs and scapulae. Partial or complete disarticulation of the lower limbs follows. The last skeletal elements to be separated are the vertebrae. Canids can scatter remains over a radius of 10 miles in open country, less in wooded areas. However, there is a great deal of variability in the extent of carnivore scavenging of accessible bodies and the time frame within which the sequence takes place. Variables include the number of animals and how hungry they may be, and factors affecting the preservation of the body. Other things being equal, carnivore activity is more extensive in cooler than hotter weather. Probably this stems from the slower decomposition in cool or cold weather. Scavengers may feed, leave, and return several times before the flesh becomes too putrid for consumption. It is the same principle as keeping meat in the refrigerator.

Conventional wisdom has held that domestic pets scavenge their owners only in desperation when pet food supplies run out. However, there is accumulating evidence that pets such as dogs, cats, and hamsters, may scavenge theirs owners' bodies in the presence of dishes of pet food and water, and sometimes within minutes of the owner's death (Rothschild and Schneider, 1997; Rodolph *et al.*, 1995; Tsokos *et al.*, 1999). The motivations for such depredations by pets are matters of speculation, but the fact does prompt one to look at Spot, Fluffy, and Squeaky in a new light.

Discriminating effects of animal activity from criminal activity is important, but is achievable in most cases with reasonable amounts of training (Blumenschine *et al.*, 1996). However, perimortem open wounds attract carnivores as well as insects, and hungry animals can disguise or completely obliterate evidence pertaining to the cause of death. Nevertheless, attention to features of animal activity may inform recovery efforts, estimates of elapsed time since death, and circumstances surrounding the death and deposition of the body.

Cremation

The cremation of bodies may be accidental, professional, or amateur. The forensic anthropologist may become involved via criminal or civil law. In the latter case, the issue often centers about professional crematories and/ or mortuary services and usually involves disputes as to the identity of the individual represented by the cremains or the completeness of the cremains. In some cases the number of individuals represented in returned "ashes" or whether the remains are partially or totally nonhuman is disputed. In at least one case the equal apportionment between the divorced and warring parents of the cremated remains of a deceased daughter was under contention. In such cases the estimated weight of the cremated remains is key. Bass and Jantz (2004) present the best data to date on cremation weights.

Modern crematoria generally fire at temperatures of approximately 1600°F, or 900°C. An overview of modern crematory practices can be found in Murad (1998) and Maples and Browning (1994). A popular belief holds that cremains taken from the retort (firing chamber) look like fireplace or cigar ashes, but in fact there are many portions of the skeleton that are still relatively intact and clearly identifiable as human (Fig. 10.4). In many cases metal remnants of dental and surgical procedures accompany these remains, and small pieces may survive any subsequent pulverization to end up in the urn. Such artifacts can be a big help in attempts to establish personal

Figure 10.4 Large element fragments in remains taken from a crematory retort, but not pulverized.

identification (Warren and Schultz, 2002). In most cases, the retort cremains are cleaned of large metal objects such as artificial joints and then pulverized to produce the "ashes", leaving only very small bone fragments. Thoroughly cremated bone is extremely friable because of the essentially complete loss of bone collagen, so even without a processor it may be easily broken into myriad small pieces. It can be the ultimate reconstruction nightmare.

Fire victims and bodies subjected to attempts at disposal or thwarting identification can undergo a great deal more variation in incineration conditions. The amount of information that can be gleaned from such remains depends on the circumstances.

Has the Body Been Burned?   This is such a basic question, yet the answer not always obvious, especially if the fire was of low intensity and short duration. The color of burned bone depends on temperature and length of exposure to the flame (Hegler, 1984; Buikstra and Swengle, 1989; Mayne Correia, 1997). The first color change to yellow-brown results from cooking the bone oils and fat at low temperature; there is little change in the weight and consistency. A blue-black color comes as organic components are destroyed and the bone is carbonized in a reducing (oxygen-starved) state. Prolonged heating at high temperature produces the final gray to white "calcined" stage when all the organic components have been destroyed. A single body, or even a single bone, may display multiple colors, reflecting different microenvironments within the cremation site.

Sun bleaching may mimic the appearance of the calcined stage, at least superficially. Far subtler is the discrimination of carbonized bone and bone stained black by soil minerals or decomposing organic material. A portable infrared mineral analyzer (PIMA) is a quick and nondestructive instrument for resolving the burned vs stained issue (Klepinger and Wisseman, 2002). This instrument was designed for field geology, but has served archaeological inquiries as well, especially in ceramics. PIMA spectra depict short-wave infrared harmonics of bending and stretching modes of molecular bonds, usually within crystals. Surprisingly, the spectrum of bone results primarily from the collagen phase, rather than the expected apatite phase. Archaeological bone may retain the collagen features and closely resemble modern bone. Cremated bones, both archaeological and modern, lose their distinctive collagen peaks. The PIMA spectrum has distinguished charred archaeological bone from black-stained bone from the same site. Even the low-temperature charring of archaeological cremation erased the distinctive collagen peaks (see Fig. 10.5). Fires set out of doors to dispose of bodies typically share low-temperature and low-oxygen characteristics with archaeological cremations.

Fracturing   The condition of bones prior to incineration can be reflected in the cracking pattern. Bones may be fleshed, green (recently defleshed and still oily), or dry. The fractures in bone produced by burning are caused by the loss of water (Shipman *et al.*, 1984), so the fluid content of the bone prior to burning is the major determinant of the fracture pattern. In a study in which they burned eight femora in each of the three condition categories (fleshed, green, dry), Buikstra and Swegle (1989) found that dry bones were, indeed, the easiest to distinguish post-incineration. The dry specimens had shallow longitudinal fissures extending along the length, and if transverse cracks occurred (rarely), they too were shallow. On the other hand, when fleshed and green bones were burned, deep transverse cracks occurred, often accompanied by deep longitudinal fissures. There were only a few key differences between fleshed and green. Diagnostic of fleshed bone were "short curved cracks forming a concentric pattern just above the inter-condylar fossa" (p. 252) in the popliteal region. This pattern is characteristic of burning fleshed long bone, and could also be described as a nested chevron or nested parabola pattern. None of Buikstra and Swegle's green bones had this pattern. Not unexpectedly, the transverse cracks were deeper and more common in the fleshed bone.

Fracturing can occur in the absence of burning by exposure to direct sun or other conditions that produce rapid loss of water. Weathering and burning can produce both cortex exfoliation and flaking.

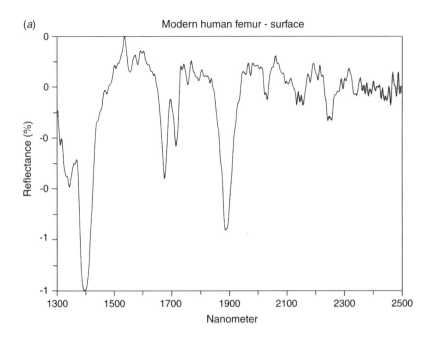

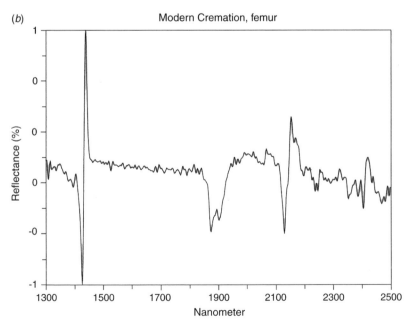

Figure 10.5 PIMA spectra of the surfaces of modern and archaeological femora show the characteristic twin collagen peaks surrounding 1700 nm. In both the modern commercial cremation and the low-temperature archaeological cremation the twin peaks disappear.

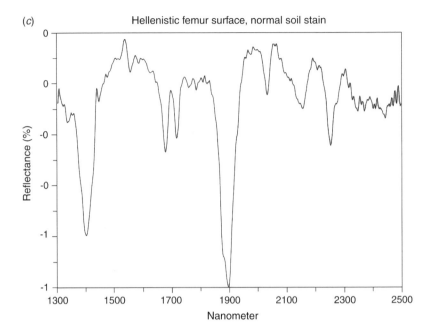

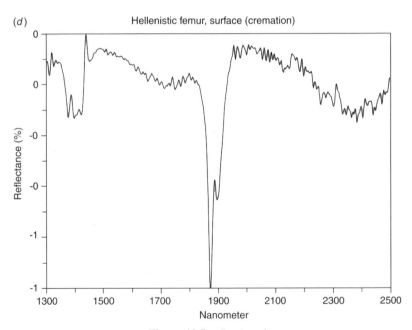

Figure 10.5 *Continued.*

Bone of the cranial vault is minimally protected by soft tissue and shows cracking and even delamination of the outer table early on (Hegler, 1984). The idea that, in an intense fire, the skull may explode when intracranial fluids expand rapidly (Bass, 1984) has been a long-held item of conventional wisdom. However, it has recently been refuted by Pope and Smith (2004), who attribute the skull fragmentation to collapsed debris and fire-fighting and handling methods.

Herman and Bennett (1999) found that sharp force trauma (scalpel, knife, saws) remained visible and recognizable following burning, but gunshot wounds were not. Blunt and spiral fractures were difficult to distinguish and required careful examination to be recognized. However, Pope and Smith (2004), in a study of burned cadaver heads, found that identifiers of ballistic, blunt force, and sharp force trauma all survived the incineration process.

Bone Shrinkage   The effect of incineration on bone is dependent on the temperature and duration of firing. There is a general agreement that gross shrinkage is on the order of 1–2 percent when temperatures are below the 700–800°C range and, therefore, not a significant deterrent to basic osteological analysis (Stewart, 1979a; Holland, 1989; Mayne Correia, 1997). However, at a temperature of 800°C or higher shrinkage can be very marked, up to 25 percent in rare cases (Hegler, 1984). High-temperature shrinkage is of sufficient magnitude to compromise metric discriminations of sex. Stature and juvenile age could also be underestimated.

The effect of burning at various temperatures on the size of microscopic features such as osteons is not entirely clear and may be very sensitive to a variety of conditions (Bradtmiller and Buikstra, 1984; Nelson, 1992). The effect of shrinkage, or perhaps sometimes expansion, of microscopic features and the integrity of the subperiosteal surface must be carefully evaluated before attempting microscopic aging techniques. The very brittle cremated bone must also be stabilized and strengthened prior to thin sectioning, so the microscopic aging methods become less accurate and more labor intensive. Quatrehomme *et al.* (1998) have shown that there is a correlation, although not perfect, between fire temperature and the appearance of microscopic features.

Dismemberment

A variety of motivations can prompt the dismemberment of a body. Three of the most popular are: (1) to stymie identification by odontology and dermatoglyphics by removal of the head, hands, and feet; (2) to enable the placement of the body into a specific container; and (3) mutilation of the corpse for emotional reasons. Detailed and well-illustrated presentations of aspects of the topic are Reichs (1998), Symes *et al.* (1998, 2002) and Houck (1998).

The usual instruments for the job are saws (manual and power), knives, and axes, although a heavy-duty wood chipper has been used to produce the ultimate dismemberment. Although much has been made, especially in dramas, of the disjointing of a corpse as betraying a special knowledge of human anatomy that cutting away from the joints does not suggest, the knowledge profiling of the perpetrator is probably overdrawn. After all, basic knowledge of human joints is not an esoteric science and not required for tidy disjointing.

It is usually possible to broadly characterize the tool used by examining the kerfs (blade marks) left on the recovered bone. False starts are cuts into the bone, but not all the way through. False start kerfs have floors that reveal something about the implement responsible for the kerf. False start kerfs from autopsy saws are common, and every worker should become familiar with the width and the flat-floored notch cross section that typifies the autopsy saw. False starts from power saws tend to go deeper than those from hand saws. A breakaway spur—a protruding piece of bone at the bottom or end of a cut where the final separation of the pieces took place—may occur when the bone is sawed all the way through. Both sides of a through-and-through cut should be examined, because the striae offer clues about the type of saw, nature of the saw teeth, and direction of cut.

Knife cutting differs from saw cutting in that the kerf floor is usually V-shaped, and the kerf is narrower than saw cuts and may even be narrower than the blade that produced it. There is less bone wastage (analogous to saw dust) with a knife than with a saw, so separated ends fit more snugly and the reconstructed bone is closer to the original dimensions. Axe cuts also leave V-shaped kerf floors, but axe chopping creates at lot more wastage from chipped-off debris, and the blades are usually much broader.

Decapitation by knife usually occurs at the level of the fourth or fifth cervical vertebra, but may be a vertebra above or below. Only a portion of a severed vertebra, along with the vertebrae superior to it, may be present with the skull, the other portion remaining with the torso. Other cervical vertebrae may show cut marks. Decapitation by saw is more variable and may remove a slice of the cranial base.

Ritual Use of Skeletal Material

The category of ritual or ceremonial use includes the taking of trophy heads in wartime, grave desecration for obtaining skeletal material (usually skulls), and use of skeletal parts for serious or frivolous rites by mainstream fraternal organizations on and off college campuses. In the case of skeletal use by

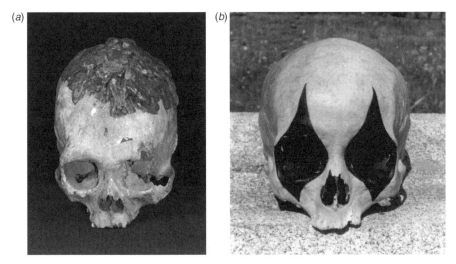

Figure 10.6   (*a*) Trophy skull with residual candle wax. (*b*) Painted skull of a woman from a desecrated old mausoleum.

fraternal organizations, the material may have been legally purchased, stolen from schools or museums, or looted from graves. Skeletal material once used in rituals may be carelessly discarded years later, only to cause concern or confusion when later discovered. Skeletal material used in ritual often has been painted, displays writing not typical of professional curation, and/or has adherent candle wax (Fig. 10.6), although some trophy skulls have no modifications.

The first question regarding the discovery of this material is one of origin: is this a matter of forensic interest, and is the recovery site a crime scene? Museum specimens should have an accession number. Commercially prepared material often has drill holes, wires, autopsy cuts, fasteners, some of which may be obviously antique; more recent material has usually been bleached, while older material may not have been. Any teeth still in a skull can be helpful in distinguishing archaeological, early historical and post-nineteenth-century dates of origin. However, the possibility that the skull could be from a recent person who did not consume a modern Western diet cannot be totally dismissed out of hand. Twentieth-century war trophy skulls are typically male and of East Asian origin. Of course, writing on the skulls may be of help.

11

PROFESSIONALISM, ETHICS, AND THE EXPERT WITNESS

Professional conduct, ethics, and the role of the expert witness are not synonymous, or even largely coincident, but these three facets of forensic science are so intertwined that their treatment fits agreeably into a single chapter, and professionalism encompasses the other two. The significant territorial overlap between ethics and expert testimony dictates more back and forth topic visitation than the headings would imply. Much of forensic anthropology's professional code is held in common with the rest of the forensic sciences.

Galloway *et al.* (1990) have provided an excellent review of these topics for the anthropologist. Although some changing aspects of law and culture have impacted the forensics sciences, the major messages of this review are fundamental to forensic practice and remain valid. A surprising change has been the rise to prominent visibility of forensic sciences and crime scene investigation in popular culture. Following the high-profile televised coverage of the O. J. Simpson trial, a plethora of documentary-style forensic programs appeared on several networks. These shows did contribute to an increasing public awareness of forensic anthropology; the focus, however, was overwhelmingly on successful investigations. Less positive consequences for the field derived from the fictional television programs, which have fostered unrealistic expectations in many viewers. In procedural protocol, scope of scientific specialties, and often-ludicrous visuals,

Fundamentals of Forensic Anthropology, by Linda L. Klepinger
Copyright © 2006 John Wiley & Sons, Inc.

scientific integrity was sacrificed to plot line. The consequences for professionals are not trivial. According to some prosecutors, juries are becoming impatient with scientific explanation and intolerant of limitations to the witness's conclusions. They increasingly express the belief that the expert must not be very good because they can do that sort of thing on television.

The popularity of forensics has also impacted dealing with the media. The general rule for anthropologists is to deflect inquiries to whomever is directing the investigation or to whatever agency requested services—unless these people specifically request that the anthropologist respond to the press. They rarely make such a request. Those who are used to dealing with the media are far less likely to compromise an investigation with a premature assessment or disclosure. However, circumspection on the part of the anthropologist comes with some negative side effects. Just about every local television station and newspaper wants an interview—if not about the current case then an extended description of the field of forensic anthropology. Given the choice of several long interviews, calling a press conference, repeatedly declining or not returning calls, most workers pick the last option. At this point the expert should prepare for some less-than-flattering nuance in the press about his (or her) expediency or forthrightness.

THE EXPERT WITNESS

Expert testimony is admissible when the subject matter is sufficiently complex that it lies beyond the experience of the average person. The purpose of the expert testimony is to provide understanding to fact finders (jurors or judge) of a subject involving highly technical knowledge. Expert testimony is unnecessary, and may be inadmissible, if the average juror is capable of comprehending the evidence without technical assistance. The expert is a person who by skill, education, or experience possesses a specialized knowledge, beyond that of the lay person, on a factual matter at issue. In contrast to the fact witness, the expert witness may testify to his own opinion based upon facts found in the record of the case. Expert opinion may be based on personal knowledge, but is not limited to that; testimony can be based on information derived from scientific literature of all kinds. The expert is not required to produce samples or apparatus in court (MacHovel, 1987; Lubet, 1998; Rossi, 1991). The competence of the expert witness means that the qualifications of the expert must relate to the matter on which he offers his opinion. The relative weight to be given to expert competency and opinion is a matter for the jury to decide.

Standards and Credentials for Expert Testimony

Standards for the admissibility of scientific evidence and expert testimony in the courts are evolving. Although the criteria for acceptance of forensic science are not yet uniform across all courts, the trend is clear. The bar is being raised.

Until 1993 the general acceptance test for scientific evidence was based on the 1923 decision of the United States Court of Appeals for the District of Columbia, *Frye v. United States.* In the *Frye* case the issue the appeals court reaffirmed was the trial court's refusal to admit evidence based on a precursor to the polygraph lie detector. The guideline established by *Frye* can be roughly summarized that the theory and instrument or technique have gained general acceptance within the relevant scientific circles and that the method has been properly applied (Black, 1988). Over the next several decades the increasing evocation of scientific evidence in both criminal and civil cases revealed weaknesses in the *Frye* standard, including lax evaluation of the theory or reasoning according to scientific standards (Foster *et al.*, 1993).

In 1993 the United States Supreme Court recognized the inadequacy of the general acceptance rule (the *Frye* standard) as the sole test for the admissibility of scientific testimony and ruled that in federal courts admissibility would be based on the Federal Rules of Evidence—Rule 702. The decision was on a toxic tort case, *Daubert v. Merrell Dow Pharmaceuticals, Inc.*, in which it was alleged that the drug Bendectin, then a popular prescription for relieving morning sickness during pregnancy, had caused serious birth defects (Mervis, 1993; Foster *et al.*, 1993). The gist of the *Daubert* ruling is that a scientific conclusion must be based on the scientific method and be relevant—that is tending to prove or disprove a fact being considered in the case. The *Daubert* decision draws a set of guidelines for judges to apply in deciding whether scientific evidence is sound and therefore admissible (Gold *et al.*, 1993). While "general acceptance" can still be a consideration, there are other factors that have a bearing. Is the theory or technique invoked testable, and has it been tested? Has it been published in a peer-reviewed forum? And what is the known or potential error rate for a technique? In effect, *Daubert* has directed federal judges to serve as gatekeepers for forensic and scientific evidence, the validity of which should be based on scientific principles.

Currently the *Daubert* guidelines are mandatory for federal courts. Some states have adopted these criteria, but other state courts continue to follow the *Frye* test. Despite the fact that the *Daubert* mandate is not universal, the fallout from the decision continues to impact forensic sciences' business-as-usual and has major implications for forensic anthropology.

Whereas DNA evidence has undergone intense scrutiny, other forensic analyses have tended to rely on expert inference taken at face value. For instance, legal identity based on fingerprint characteristics has no universal standard for acceptance or estimates of error rates, and there has been considerable room for disagreement when a partial print from a crime scene has been matched to a full print from a database. The 16 January 2002 *Christian Science Monitor* reported that a federal judge excluded a fingerprint expert's testimony that a defendant's fingerprints definitely matched those found at a crime scene. The judge who excluded the fingerprint testimony later reversed his own decision by reaching the astonishing conclusion that forensic science was a specialty, not a science (Faigman, 2002). This reversal of ruling and some other legal statements seem to call into question the ability of some scientifically naive lawyers and judges to appreciate the scientific approach of testing hypotheses (Faigman, 2002). Some courts have even found the scientific issue to be irrelevant. One federal appeals court ruled that science does not matter in issues of law, only whether the fact-finder "found sufficient evidence of causation in a legal sense" (Ayala and Black, 1993: 230). According to the same *Christian Science Monitor* article that reported the exclusion of fingerprint testimony, other recent court decisions have excluded testimony from handwriting and knife-mark experts. The latter is hitting very close to home. It is not much of a stretch to interpret this as a warning to forensic anthropologists. Expert testimony based on experience and knowledge may no longer be sufficient. Experts should be prepared to address inquiries as to whether their methods can be or have been tested, and about their methodology's peer review and publication, error rates, and degree of acceptance in the field. Christensen (2004) has explored the implications of the changing testimony standards initiated by *Daubert* to the use of frontal sinus morphology in personal identification.

Confusion and inconsistency have not been eliminated, but one can applaud efforts to get "junk science" out of the courts. The increasing reliance on scientific evidence is matched, if not surpassed, by public fascination with forensics. All of this contributes to the increasingly lucrative enterprise of being an expert witness. Although glossy credentials may no longer carry the day in the face of questionable scientific validity, establishing who really is or is not an expert remains a top consideration. Legitimate and prestigious organizations, such as the American Association for the Advancement of Science and the American Academy of Forensic Sciences and its affiliated professional certification boards, have taken up the challenge of identifying genuine experts on whom the courts may rely, but as potential expert witnesses rush to bolster their resumes, less legitimate entrepreneurs have perceived an opportunity in the credentialing business. A case in point is the American College of Forensic Examiners (formerly the American Board of Forensic Examiners) whose slip-shod, fee-focused approach to board certification has been well documented (Hansen, 2000). Their whole approach trivializes the words "expert" and "ethics". Unfortunately, many attorneys who become involved in criminal or civil litigation are not aware of the distinctions between credentialing organizations and what such distinctions signify. As a result, juries are led to believe or left to assume that all certifications and professional memberships vouch for similar levels of expertise. Increased prominence of forensic sciences and legal standards for expert witnesses will alleviate the more flagrant misrepresentations.

While forensic anthropology has not been a notable target of bogus credentialing boards, some individuals with substandard training, who would not be deemed experts by their peers, have been accepted to testify as experts in court. The days of such easy acceptance may well dwindling, but in the future, experience, extensive training, and even board certification may not suffice by themselves. Witnesses will have to evaluate the reliability of their methodologies, errors and all.

Some Practical Issues

Expert witnesses may be called in both civil and criminal actions. Forensic anthropologists are involved primarily, though not exclusively, in criminal proceedings. Although much of what is written about expert testimony is directed toward civil trials, most of the points apply equally well to criminal law.

Most attorneys follow a typical procedure in beginning direct questioning in order to establish expertise:

- name;
- current employment;
- employment history;
- educational background, including degrees;
- professional activity including teaching, research, and publication in forensic anthropology;
- definition of terms "physical anthropology" and "forensic anthropology";
- membership in relevant professional organizations;
- relevant licensure or certifications.

On either direct or cross-examination the witness will almost certainly be asked the number of prior trials, and on behalf of which side. In criminal trials forensic anthropologists are more frequently called by the prosecution than by the defense. However, there can be a negative impact on the jury if the witness has never testified for the defense, since this could imply bias or a tendency of the witness to be a "hired gun" for the prosecution.

Usually, prior to trial are requests from the opposing side to inspect all tangible materials involved in the course of working on the case. This process of discovery can list almost all documents created by the expert or used by the expert in forming an opinion (Lubet, 1998; Rossi, 1991; Schwarzer and Cecil, 2000). For anthropologists this list can include the analysis report, notes, data collected, and presumably, even citations and cited material.

Related pretrial procedures that are sometimes used include interrogatories and depositions (MacHovel, 1987). Interrogatories are written answers, usually given under oath, to a set of written questions submitted by the opposing lawyer. Depositions are oral questions asked under oath by the lawyers from both sides. Depositions may also be used when the expert, for some reason, cannot appear to testify in court. Depositions are recorded, and a transcript is submitted to the witness for corrections.

The witness should be prepared to establish a clear chain of custody with dates and times, and to explain the circumstances of his or her involvement in the case. As a rule, the witness is allowed to consult notes or other written material before responding to questions involving details of the analysis. Sometimes a witness will be asked questions out of the blue that appear to be irrelevant to the facts at issue. Such questions may relate to previous testimony or be an attempt by the opposing attorney to discredit the witness's expertise or to minimize the expert's impact on the jury. Even if asked to discourse at some length about, say, Cro Magnon, as was a colleague of mine in a murder trial, the expert should always be cooperative. For those seeking information on how to be a persuasive expert witness, several books and expert witness training courses teach form, rather than substance, of testimony.

Finally, absolute immunity from lawsuit for a witness's trial or pretrial testimony may not always hold (Starrs, 2002). Experts can and have faced malpractice suits. One measure of protection, according to Starrs, may be to request a subpoena, making testimony compulsory. There is no immunity from nonfrivolous malpractice suits for analyses and opinions not involving testimony.

ETHICS

In 1999 an article by a chemist at University of Illinois appeared in a campus newspaper He had been a court-appointed independent expert witness under Federal Court Rule 706. At issue in the civil dispute was the scientific interpretation of a patent for an ultrasonic-assisted liposuction invention. The chemist stated (Suslick, 1999: 7), "While I've served as an expert witness before, I'd never been a Rule 706 expert before. As an expert witness for either the defendant or the plaintiff the job is like being a hired gun in an old western. As a court-appointed expert, however, it's a lot more like being a deputy sheriff. My role was to act as a technical arbitrator between conflicting expert witness testimony in the interpretation of a patent." What's amiss with this statement? The perception of where a scientist's loyalties lie is erroneous. The prime directive for the scientific witness is to collect, analyze, and interpret all pertinent data as if for scientific publication subject to peer assessment. The mission of the scientist is the same, regardless of whether his services have been engaged by one of the opposing sides or by the court as an independent expert witness; this principle holds whether the proceeding is criminal or civil.

Fees for services should have absolutely no bearing on the expert's conclusions. Fees for the services of expert witnesses are the rule rather than the exception, unless such services are considered to be encompassed by the witness's primary employment. The anthropologist's real clients are the discipline and the deceased; this duel clientele does not constitute a conflict of interest. Experts should avoid fees contingent upon the outcome of the case. Experts should also avoid accepting excessive fees, although this caveat rarely, if ever, affects anthropologists. Contingency or excessive fees lend an aura of bias and may promote a temptation to bias, although opposing attorneys may try to portray it that way no matter how the fees are arranged.

Balanced reports and testimony can face subtle assault. For example, sometimes law enforcement officers and prosecuting attorneys will emphasize to the expert the heinousness of the crime, the suffering of the victim, and the past wrong-doing of the defendant in the hope that the expert witness will strengthen the certainty of conclusions and persuasiveness of testimony. The expert's degree of certainty can be very salient to the jury, but the degree of certainty is what it is; advocacy is the role of the attorney, not the expert witness.

Ethical responsibilities of the expert witness extend to maintaining honesty in regard to qualifications and staying within an appropriate area of expertise (as judged by professional peers), using analytical methods of proven reliability, and being open about the findings (Hollien, 1990). Problems may also arise in regard to a nontestifying expert, for instance, one who may help plan strategy or assist an attorney in preparing cross-examination or impeachment of experts testifying for the other side. Within the legal system these are considered to be ethical behaviors, but there does seem to be substantial confusion about the proper role of expert consultants (Hollien, 1990).

SCIENCE IN THE COURTROOM: TWO UNFORTUNATE EXAMPLES

When Good Science is not Presented

One of the more egregious examples of the breakdown of professionalism and ethics in the forensic sciences involved Dr Louise Robbins, Associate Professor of Anthropology at the University of North Carolina, Greensboro. The problems, which received significant national media attention, involved analyses of footprint and footwear evidence. The analysis of footwear impressions and of footprints (not involving dermatoglyphic features) had not previously constituted a skill within the traditional bailiwick of forensic anthropology, but it became a specialty for Robbins. Challenges to Robbins' testimony in appellate court are summarized in Moenssens *et al.* (1995). In one California case she testified that the same person who wore the defendant's shoes wore the shoes found at a gravesite. This was determined by comparing foot impressions on the insoles of the shoes, and also by comparing the insole impressions to inked foot impressions of the defendant. Robbins explained her methodology as one using a grid system with many points of measurement designed to analyze the pressure points of the feet. In another case she claimed that a crime scene footwear impression was made by the defendant's foot to the exclusion of all others.

Receiving much attention was the trial of three men accused of the 1983 rape and murder of a 10-year-old girl in Naperville, Illinois. Summaries of the major events of the case and of the legal convolutions are found in Moessens *et al.* (1995); *Chicago Tribune* 6 and 18 April 1986 and 5 November 1995; and *Chicago Sun-Times* 6 March 1987 and 9 January 1996.

In 1983 the girl was abducted while home alone with the flu. Two days later her body was found. A little more than a year later Rolando Cruz, Alejandro Hernandez, and Steven Buckley, all of neighboring Aurora, were indicted for that rape and murder. About 2 months later (2 May 1984), Brian Dugan was arrested for burglary in another town and was released later that same month. In less than a month from Dugan's release a northern Illinois woman was raped and murdered. In February of 1985 Cruz and Hernandez were convicted of the Naperville girl's murder. Because the jury had deadlocked on Buckley, a retrial for him was scheduled. In the absence of any witnesses to the crime, a bootprint on the door of the girl's house assumed considerable importance for prosecuting the case. Three separate experts at state and county forensic laboratories could not declare a match of the bootprint to Buckley's boots. As a consequence, the DuPage County State's Attorney's Office sought an expert who would have proper fealty to their cause—thus following the advice proffered to trial lawyers: "So, as you labor to assemble your case, the strength of the scientific support for an expert's testimony is quite secondary. It is the strength of the expert's support for *your* position that comes first" (Huber, 1991: 18, emphasis in the original). Louise Robbins positively identified the bootprint left on the door when the killer(s) broke in to burglarize the house as Buckley's.

A sense of the basis for Robbins' conclusion can be gleaned from excerpts from the Buckley, Cruz, and Hernandez trial transcript from the afternoon of 28 January 1985. The most concise statements of Robbins' theory and methodology come from her cross-examination by defense attorney Gary Johnson:

From p. 94:

Q   It's your theory that the wear patterns that we all have on the bottoms of our shoes are unique to the individual; is that correct?

A   That is correct, sir.

Q   So stated another way, there is nobody else in the world who has a shoe wear pattern like I do other than me?

A   That is right, sir.

From p. 104:

Q   And with regard to the theory that you've got that wear patterns are unique to the individual, are you saying that they are of the same ilk as fingerprints are to the individual?

A   They are distinctive to the individual in a comparable way in that it's a combination of features, genetic, but with the wear patterning, the life experiences of the individual, which is another factor. They're comparable in a way to fingerprints.

Q   So you are saying that they are as unique as fingerprints are; that Gary Johnson's wear on the bottom of his shoes is as unique to him as his right index finger fingerprint?

A   Yes, sir.

From pp. 134 and 135:

Q   And it's based on these hundred prints that you testified that you have that you have come to your conclusion that these shoeprints, the wear patterns on the bottoms of shoeprints, are unique to the person along the same lines as a fingerprint?

A   It's not just the hundred. I examine shoeprints and bottoms of shoes whenever I can.

Q   Under what circumstances do you examine shoeprints whenever you can?

A   I stop students on campus.

Q   And you ask them to lift up their feet and you check out the bottoms of their feet?

A   Especially when they walk across an area, as I showed in the first slide, in that one particular area in particular.

Q   When you stop these students, do you take photographs of the bottom of their feet?

A   No, sir.

Q   Do you measure wear patterns, whether it be on the ball of the foot, or the heel of the foot, measure the wear patterns?

A   No, sir.

Q   So, therefore, it's safe to say when you stop somebody at the University of North Carolina, Greensboro, or wherever you are when you stop somebody, you don't actually record in any way any of the characteristics that you checked out?

A   Other than turning—having them turn the shoe over, or I turn the shoe over, positioning it by the shoeprint that was made and then, with dividers, checkout the distribution and positioning of wear in the heel, on the rear of the heel, the outer side or inner side, depending, and then working on up the shoe that way, simply for my information.

Q   Do you record that information that you keep?

A   No, sir.

From p. 143:

Q   Can you make the conclusion solely on the wear on the heel that this heel is unique to the person, the wear on this heel?

A   The wear distribution along the length of the heel reflects the way that person uses the foot in the shoe, and therefore, is indeed unique to that person.

Q   Compared to the rest of the world? Nobody else would make a heel print like that; is that correct?

A   That's correct, sir.

On 15 March 1985 Cruz and Hernandez were sentenced to death. In early June of the same year a 7-year-old girl was raped and murdered, and Brian Dugan was arrested and later convicted for that murder and for the murder of the woman in 1984. In November Dugan confessed to killing the Naperville girl and insisted that he acted alone. Prosecutors were unconvinced by Dugan's story, as was the judge who banned it from Buckley's retrial. In June of 1986 the FBI reported that the bootprint on the door was excluded as being Buckley's (Bodziak, 2000). In February of 1987 a national panel of forensic scientists, including anthropologists, concluded Robbins' methodology to be unsound. The following month the 18-times-delayed retrial of Buckley was dropped because Robbins, dying of cancer, was unable to testify. Buckley was freed.

Many people assumed that Buckley's 1987 release would shortly be followed by the release of Cruz and Hernandez. The Illinois Supreme Court ordered retrials for Cruz and Hernandez because of previous errors in trial procedures. In January 1990 DNA tests run on sperm found on the Naperville girl's body excluded both Buckley and Hernandez as her attacker, but could not exclude either Dugan or Cruz. Subsequent retrials eventually resulted in the death sentence for Cruz and 80 years in prison for Hernandez. In 1995 DNA tests excluded Cruz from the rape and strongly implicated Dugan. By the end of 1995 both Cruz and Hernandez had been released—more than 11 years after their indictment.

Where did the forensic anthropologist go wrong and contribute to a serious failing in the justice system? Louise Robbins strayed from standards of professionalism and ethics in the following ways:

- She extended her espoused area of expertise beyond that regularly subsumed by forensic anthropology. Footwear impression is not an area in which anthropologists receive formal training, and it trespasses on the territory of other specialists.
- She did not employ a methodology or theory generally accepted in the field or followed by anyone else. Certainly it is not always easy to distinguish trail-blazing procedures from fringe science. However, in this case other scientists would be challenged to understand, much less approve of, her heterodox procedures and assertions. Her book (Robbins, 1985), in press at the time of her trial testimony, is not enlightening in this regard. The courtroom is an appropriate setting for Carl Sagan's caution that extraordinary claims demand extraordinary proofs.
- Consciously or unconsciously she biased her conclusions to favor the cause of her immediate employer. This tendency was widely recognized by many attorneys.

There may have been extenuating health circumstances influencing Robbins' breach of professional conduct standards. Moreover, officers of the court were far from blameless in this outrageous course of events. It is hard to imagine how Robbins' methodology was deemed to have satisfied the *Frye* standard of general acceptance, the standard for admissibility at the time. The main point of this recounting is to illustrate how lives literally may hang in balance if professional ethics fall away.

When Good Science is Ignored

Sometimes the expert witness enjoys the satisfaction of explaining and interpreting a straightforward scientific fact with great certainty, but leading triers of fact to an incontrovertible conclusion is, apparently, sometimes irrelevant to the outcome.

Berry v. Chaplin is a case in point (Huber, 1991). In 1943 a young woman, Joan Berry, gave birth to a daughter she named Carol Ann. Berry claimed the actor Charlie Chaplin, a rich, famous, middle-aged, reputed womanizer, had fathered her daughter during one of four romantic trysts they had shared the previous December. Chaplin, who did not deny that there had been an earlier affair, did deny that there had been any intimate encounter after March of 1942. Miss Berry sued Chaplin for child support. During the trial evidence came forth linking Berry to two, possibly three, other men around the time frame for Carol Ann's conception. On the evidence so far Chaplin *could* have been the father, but was not conclusively implicated in the paternity. Scientific tests offered definitive evidence on the validity of the paternity claim.

Since Landsteiner's 1901 discovery of the ABO blood groups, the genetics of the A and B antigens had been characterized. The ABO blood type system comprises three major alleles. Alleles A and B are both dominant to allele O, and A and B are codominant to each other. Therefore an individual with blood type A (the phenotype) may have parental alleles A and A, or A and O (the genotypes). Similarly, blood type B may result from either B and B, or B and O genotypes. An individual with type AB blood must have received the A allele from one parent and the B allele from the other parent. Because the O allele is recessive to both A and B, an individual with type O blood must have received an O allele from both parents, that is, must be homozygous for the O allele. Joan Berry had blood type A, and baby Carol Ann had blood type B. Carol Ann's father had to be either blood type B or type AB. Charlie Chaplin had type O blood. Three physicians testified that Chaplin could not have been the biological father of the baby, but to no avail. The jury found in favor of Miss Berry. An appeal court upheld the verdict with one judge decrying the failure of the courts to utilize science in depicting the truth about the fact in question.

Why the trial jury and a majority of an appellate court chose to ignore uncontested expert testimony about a scientific fact that was not beyond the understanding of the average instructed person is a matter of speculation. A variety of reasons can contribute to "fact-finders" electing to side with facts as they feel they should be, as opposed to facts as they are. Sometimes neither the science nor the expert is wanting, but justice is still not served.

12

GENETICS AND DNA

In the mid-1990s I was asked to consult on the exhumation of a body. Eighteen years previously the badly decomposed remains of a young male with a gunshot entry wound through the occipital bone had been identified on the basis of dental records. Recently, a suspect had been arrested for the 18-year-old murder, and his attorney was disputing the original identification of the corpse. The problem was that the only records of that original identification had been based on one dentist's description of 13 notable dental characteristics that had been described over the telephone to the personal dentist of the alleged victim. No copies of any part of the alleged victim's dental records had been placed in the coroner's files, and the victim's dentist had long since left the area and destroyed all of his deceased patients' records. In fact, neither dentist was available for testimony, and the only evidence that pertained to the identification was a written notation of the 13 missing or restored teeth and a written report of the telephone conversation and orally agreed upon identity. The state's attorney's office was not confident that such evidence of identification would carry the day in court, and the primary purpose of the exhumation was to acquire a sample of DNA from the skeletal remains in order to confirm the identification. I asked whose DNA would be used for comparison with any recovered 18-year-old DNA and was told that they had located the father and the ex-wife of the presumed victim. Interesting.

Fundamentals of Forensic Anthropology, by Linda L. Klepinger
Copyright © 2006 John Wiley & Sons, Inc.

The point of this story is to show that, although DNA analysis itself is in the bailiwick of other forensic scientists, anthropologists would do well to be acquainted with the basics of forensic serology and DNA analysis; they may have to offer advice on appropriate sampling.

SEROLOGY AND MENDELIAN GENETICS

Until the mid-decade 1980s twentieth-century forensic serology relied upon the analysis of Mendelian alleles (alternative forms of the same gene) that defined an ever-growing series of blood group markers and biochemical systems. In most cases samples were taken of blood or semen from the living or very recently deceased. The genetic analysis could be applied to fairly fresh corpses for identification of the deceased, but more often it served to characterize an assailant or provide a probability of, or exclusion of, paternity. The more blood group or biochemical loci that could be tested, the more precisely the laboratory results could approach the distinctive qualities of the individual who, deliberately or not, supplied the sample.

The frequency of individuals possessing a defined set of genetic markers is computed by simply multiplying the appropriate population frequencies of each allele together. Taking an example of Caucasian Californians (Grunbaum et al., 1978), 48.2 percent are type O blood, and 20.8 percent are Rh negative, so $0.482 \times 0.208 = 0.100$ or 10 percent of that population are type O negative. If one expands these data to include 57 possible systems (ignoring any problems of laboratory error), the pinpointing of nonexcluded individuals can boast probabilities in the high 90s (Chakraborty et al., 1974). However, aside from high-profile cases of disputed parentage, such batteries of tests were rarely feasible or even possible. The protein polymorphisms to be tested degraded quickly once outside a living body, so only a few were really forensically useful in identifying assailants or victims, and even these quickly lost reliability after a few months.

Joseph Wambaugh's (1989) book, *The Blooding* is a factual account of the rape–murders of two teenage girls in Leicestershire, England in November 1983 and July 1986 and provides a glimpse of serological investigation as practiced in the mid-1980s (p. 39):

> The laboratory analysis offered the murder squad its first positive clue. The report showed that the killer had, after ejaculating prematurely, managed to penetrate the victim prior to death. Semen was taken from an internal labial swab and on a deep vaginal swab.

Given a phosphoglucomutase (PGM) grouping test, the semen showed strong PGM 1+ enzyme reaction. It was antigen-tested and found to contain strong amounts of Group A secretor substance.

The officers on the murder inquiry were told that only one out of ten male adults in England was in this particular blood group. The scientific label would remain the only clue they possessed. The killer was a Group A secretor, PGM 1+. Without understanding exactly what it meant, hundreds of police officers would repeat it for nearly four years: "We're looking for a PGM one-plus, 'A' secretor."

Actually there is no "secretor substance". Secretor (*Se*) is a gatekeeper allele. In a secretor ABO blood group antigens pass into extra-vascular fluids such as saliva and semen. Taking ABO, PGM, and the secretor system frequencies in England from Mourant *et al.* (1976) and PGM subgroup frequencies from Gaensslen *et al.* (1987) for "Minnesota Caucasians", which should be applicable to the Leicester area, yields the following figures. In the ABO blood group system for the Leicestershire area ($n = 75{,}166$), A $= 0.431$. In the secretor system, in the nearby Lancashire ($n = 2435$), secretors $= 0.758$. In the PGM system in England ($n = 2115$), PGM1 $= 0.585$, and in the PGM1 system subgroups ($n = 8662$), PGM 1+ $= 0.674$. The probability of an individual producing semen testing positive for A and PGM1+ would be:

$$0.431 \times 0.758 \times 0.585 \times 0.674 = 0.129 \text{ or } 12.9 \text{ percent}$$

The point of this exercise is to demonstrate the quantitative procedures and typical results for serological laboratory analysis at the dawn of the DNA revolution.

The rape–murders detailed in *The Blooding* were the first murder cases in which DNA "fingerprinting" was utilized. The technique was developed by Professor Alec Jeffreys of nearby Leicester University. A teenage boy who had confessed to one murder but not the other had been found not to be a PGM 1+, A secretor. Jeffreys' testing indicated that both rapes and presumably both murders were committed by the same person, but not the confessed murderer. Massive DNA testing of the young men of the area was instrumental in the apprehension and confession of the dual murderer, who had the memorable name of Colin Pitchfork.

FORENSIC DNA ANALYSIS

The techniques that Jeffreys devised looked at areas of nuclear DNA that displayed the most variation between individuals. During replication of certain

noncoding areas of DNA there can be stutter-like repetitions of some segments that produce hundreds of variations at each locus. Called VNTRs
(variable number of tandem repeats) the segments can be chopped into
unequal lengths when the DNA is digested by a restriction enzyme, and
hence the VNTRs are referred to as RFLPs, or restriction fragment length
polymorphisms. RFLPs produced great discrimination and could differen-
tiate contributors when more than one person contributed to the sample.
This procedure is very rarely used anymore because it is time-consuming
and requires relatively large and nondegraded samples (Kaye and
Sensabaugh, 2000).

This original DNA "fingerprinting" technique was quickly followed by
the polymerase chain reaction (PCR)-based DNA amplification that could
be applied to samples of nuclear DNA that were 10- to 500-fold smaller
than that required for RFLP (Kaye and Sensabaugh, 2000). Moreover, the
time required for laboratory results dropped significantly. The drawbacks
to PCR were that its extreme sensitivity made it capable of amplifying
tiny bits of contaminating DNA (Parsons and Weedn, 1997), it had less discriminating power than RFLP and was not as good at resolving mixtures.

The early autosomal VNTR (a.k.a. minisatellite) markers have been
eclipsed by microsatellites. These comprise short tandem repeat (STR)
units, often between one and four bases (Harvey and King, 2002). They
may be amplified by PCR and used to type deteriorated samples. Typical
STRs fall in the range of 50–350 base pairs, and gel electrophoresis can
be used to examine several DNA regions, or loci, at once. As more STR
loci are included, they can be more individualizing than the VNTR profiling
of four or five loci (Kaye and Sensabaugh, 2000; Watson, 2000). Of several
thousand known variable STR loci, about 10–15 are used in a DNA profile.
The FBI uses 13 STR loci in establishing the U.S. national DNA database
system, called CODIS (combined DNA index system; Watson, 2000).
There is tremendous variation among jurisdictions as to what sorts of con-
victions allow DNA database sample collections. In Champaign County,
Illinois, persons convicted of theft in 2003 were ordered to provide the
state with a DNA sample and pay $200 to have it processed.

The autosomal HLA genes code for human leukocyte antigens, part of the
major histocompatibility complex. Two loci have been used forensically.
The HLA-DQ locus probe has detected six alleles, and HLA-DQ typing
has a fairly long track record and was part of the DNA evidence in the
trial of O. J. Simpson. The HLA-DRB1 locus has many more alleles. HLA
genes are amenable to PCR amplification.

Nonautosomal nuclear DNA genotypes include Y-chromosome STRs and
amelogenin. Microsatellite markers on the Y-chromosome can identify a
paternal lineage. The amelogenin site is useful for establishing sex, although

there appears to be an unacceptably high failure rate in some populations (Chang *et al.*, 2003). The X chromosome has a 6 base pair deletion (106 base pairs) in the amelogenin gene in comparison with the amelogenin gene on the Y chromosome (112 base pairs), so two X-chromosomes show one band, and XY genotypes show two.

Not all human DNA resides in the cell nucleus. Some DNA is found in the cell mitochondria, the organelles that house the cellular machinery for oxidative metabolism that produces energy. Compared with the nuclear genome the mitochondrial genome is quite small—16,569 base pairs to be exact—of which a 1200 base pair region is hypervariable (Harvey and King, 2002). At first glance it would appear that this small amount could degrade to nothing very quickly, but the small genome size of mitochondrial DNA (mtDNA) is more than compensated for by its very high copy number, so that there is thousands of times more mitochondrial than nuclear DNA. Because there is so much more to begin with, mtDNA can often be retrieved from skeletal or other decomposed remains long after the nuclear DNA has dropped below an analyzable threshold. Skeletal material is among the best sources of DNA from decomposed human remains (Gaensslen *et al.*, 1994). Molars are often better than bone, especially in the event of fire, because they are somewhat protected by the mouth. Mitochondrial DNA can also be recovered from hair shafts, whereas the hair root is required for nuclear DNA.

A couple of other differences between nuclear and mitochondrial DNA are forensically salient. For one thing, mtDNA mutates so frequently that a single individual may show a mixture of variants, called heteroplasmy, not seen in nuclear DNA. Laboratories account for this by insisting that more than one sequence difference between samples be present to declare an exclusion (Harvey and King, 2002). The more important difference is in inheritance pattern. For all practical purposes inheritance of mtDNA is exclusively through the maternal lineage. Thus, mtDNA is shared between full and half-siblings who share a mother, between mother and child, between cousins whose mothers are sisters, between an individual and maternal grandmother and maternal aunts and uncles, and so forth. To return to the story of the 18-year-old murder at the beginning of this chapter, the victim's mtDNA would be the DNA most likely recovered. The man would share his mtDNA with *neither* his father *nor* (we hope!) his ex-wife. Relatives in the maternal line would need to be sampled, or the entire endeavor would be pointless.

The mtDNA is the maternal lineage counterpart of the Y-chromosome DNA. However, it can be recovered from both sexes and from more degraded tissue, so mtDNA may be recovered from male remains when Y-chromosome DNA cannot be. Although only one line of parentage would be traceable, the maternal line is often known with a greater degree of certainty than the paternal line.

LEGAL CONSIDERATIONS

The U.S. National DNA Database is being constructed from data uploaded from state databases. The full promise of DNA analyses has been compromised by several circumstances, the most prominent being the tremendous backlog of samples to be run by various government laboratories, including thousands of rape kits. Moreover, sometimes the statute of limitations has run out, or DNA profiles from outmoded techniques need to be redone for CODIS. National or large-scale emergencies can exacerbate the overload. The World Trade Center attacks added on the order of 20,000 more samples (including 13,000 bone samples) to be identified, and these often move to the front of the line. As public forensic science laboratories try simply to tread water, many cases are allotted to the private sector. Several bills aimed at funding the reduction of backlogs are pending.

On a more positive note DNA analysis has undergone intense courtroom scrutiny as a forensic science. Strenuous tests have challenged DNA technology's theoretical basis, error rate, and laboratory and collection protocols. In fact, DNA analysis has demonstrated a reliability and quality control that surpasses comparable credentials of many or most of the forensic sciences. DNA's positive track record in court does not, however, automatically translate into scientifically informed legal decision-making.

Once again, the pitfall may be statistical. Hoffrage *et al.* (2000) provide an example of a reported DNA match between a defendant and a sample recovered from a rape victim. The DNA was the only real evidence against the defendant. A testifying expert reported the frequency of the DNA profile to be, literally, one in a million, and that the test would always show a match for a person with that DNA profile. That is, the test's sensitivity was 100 percent. The reported false-positive rate was 0.003. On the basis of this evidence should the defendant be convicted? Once again we have a case of evaluating the positive predictive value of a test: given a positive test, what is the chance that the person has the implicated DNA profile? To figure this take the prevalence of the profile (1 in 1,000,000). Since this test's sensitivity is 100 percent, all who have the type will test positive. Thus, 1 in 1,000,000 will test positive because they have the profile. For the other 999,999 in a million 0.3 percent will falsely test positive. So, in this example, only one in 3000 people who test positive for the implicated DNA profile actually has that profile.

One lesson from the example is that nobody who is an expert should be allowed to get away with ignoring test error rates and stating only the frequency (prevalence) of, say one in 10 million. Such figures by themselves are potentially misleading because most people, including jurors, would draw the wrong inference with regard to guilt. In the above example the sensitivity was 100 percent, but if it were reported as 50 percent, half of the people with the sought-after profile would not be detected, even if tested. Another lesson from this exercise regards the caution that must apply to blindly screening DNA databases for matches—especially when corroborative evidence is lacking.

REFERENCES

Acsádi, Gy., and Nemeskéri, J. (1970). *History of Human Life Span and Mortality.* Budapest: Akadémiai Kiadó.

Adams, B. J., and Byrd, J. E. (2002). Interobserver variation of selected postcranial skeletal measurements. *Journal of Forensic Sciences* **47**: 1193–1202.

Aiello, L. C., and Molleson, T. (1993). Are microscopic ageing techniques more accurate than macroscopic ageing techniques? *Journal of Archaeological Science* **20**: 689–704.

Albert, A. M., and Maples, W. R. (1995). Stages of epiphyseal union for thoracic and lumber vertebral centra as a method of age determination for teenage and young adult skeletons. *Journal of Forensic Sciences* **40**: 623–633.

Anderson, M., Green, W. T., and Messner, M. B. (1963). Growth and predictions of growth in the lower extremities. *The Journal of Bone and Joint Surgery* **45-A**: 1–14.

Angel, J. L. (1969). The bases of paleodemography. *American Journal of Physical Anthropology* **30**: 427–437.

Aufderheide, A. C., and Rodriguez-Martin, C. (1998). *The Cambridge Encyclopedia of Human Paleopathology.* Cambridge: Cambridge University Press.

Ayala, F. J., and Black, B. (1993). Science and the courts. *American Scientist* **81**: 230–239.

Baker, P. T., and Newman, R. W. (1957). *The Use of Dry Bone Weights for Identification.* Quartermaster Research and Development Center, Environmental

Protection Research Division, Technical Report EP-55. Natick, MA: Headquarters Quartermaster Research and Development Command.

Baker, S. J., Gill, G. W., and Kieffer, D. H. (1990). Race and sex determination from the intercondylar notch of the distal femur. In G. W. Gill and S. Rhine (Eds), *Skeletal Attribution of Race*. Maxwell Museum of Anthropology Anthropological Papers No. 4. Albuquerque, NM: University of New Mexico Maxwell Museum of Anthropology, pp. 91–95.

Barsness, K. A., Cha, E. S., Bensard, D. D. Calkins, C. M., Partrick, D. A., Karrer, F. M., and Strain, J. D. (2003). Positive predictive value of rib fractures as an indicator of non-accidental trauma in children. *Journal of Trauma* **56**: 1107–1110.

Bass, W. M. (1984). Is it possible to consume a body completely in a fire? In T. A. Rathbun and J. E. Buikstra (Eds), *Human Identification: Case Studies in Forensic Anthropology*. Springfield, IL: Charles C. Thomas, pp. 159–107.

Bass, W. M. (1995). *Human Osteology: A Laboratory and Field Manual*, 4th edn. Columbia, MO: Missouri Archaeological Society.

Bass, W. M. III (1997). Outdoor decomposition rates in Tennessee. In W. D. Haglund and M. H. Sorg (Eds), *Forensic Taphonomy: The Postmortem Fate of Human Remains*. Boca Raton, FL: CRC Press, pp. 181–186.

Bass, W. M., and Jantz, R. L. (2004). Cremation weights in east Tennessee. *Journal of Forensic Sciences* **49**: 901–904.

Baumann, E., and O'Brien, J. (1986). The sausage factory mystery. *Chicago Tribune Magazine*, 3 August 1986, pp. 16–20.

Benfer, R. A., and McKern, T. W. (1966). The correlation of bone robusticity with the perforation of the coronoid-olecranon septum in the humerus of man. *American Journal of Physical Anthropology* **24**: 247–252.

Berrizbeitia, E. L. (1989). Sex determination with the head of the radius. *Journal of Forensic Sciences* **34**: 1206–1213.

Berryman, H. E., and Symes, S. A. (1998). Recognizing gunshot and blunt cranial trauma through fracture interpretation. In K. J. Reichs (Ed.), *Forensic Osteology: Advances in the Identification of Human Remains*, 2nd edn. Springfield, IL: Charles C. Thomas, pp. 333–352.

Berryman, H. E., Smith, O. C., and Symes, S. H. (1995). Diameter of cranial gunshot wounds as a function of bullet caliber. *Journal of Forensic Sciences* **40**: 751–754.

Black, B. (1988). Evolving legal standards for the admissibility of scientific evidence. *Science* **239**: 1508–1512.

Black, T. K. III (1978). A new method for assessing the sex of fragmentary skeletal remains: Femoral shaft circumference. *American Journal of Physical Anthropology* **48**: 227–232.

Blumenschine, R. J., Marean, C., and Capaldo, S. D. (1996). Blind tests of inter-analyst correspondence and accuracy in the identification of cut marks, percussion marks, and carnivore tooth marks on bone surfaces. *Journal of Archaeological Science* **23**: 493–507.

Bodziak, W. J. (2000). *Footwear Impression Evidence: Detection, Recovery, and Examination*, 2nd edn. Boca Raton, FL: CRC Press.

Bradtmiller, B. M, and Buikstra, J. E. (1984). Effects of burning on human bone microstructure: A preliminary study. *Journal of Forensic Sciences* **29**: 535–540.

Brooks, S. T. (1955). Skeletal age at death: The reliability of cranial and pubic age indicators. *American Journal of Physical Anthropology* **13**: 567–597.

Brooks, S., and Suchey, J. M. (1990). Skeletal age determination based on the os pubis: A comparison of the Acsádi–Nemeskérí and Suchey–Brooks methods. *Human Evolution* **5**: 227–238.

Buikstra, J. E., and Swegle, M. (1989). Bone modification due to burning: experimental evidence. In R. Bonnichsen and M. H. Sorg (Eds), *Bone Modification*. Orono, ME: University of Maine, pp. 247–258.

Buikstra, J. E., and Ubelaker, D. H. (Eds) (1994). *Standards for Data Collection from Human Skeletal Remains*. Arkansas Archaeological Survey Research Series No. 44. Fayetteville, AK: Arkansas Archaeological Survey.

Burns, K. R. (1998). Forensic anthropology and human rights issues. In K. J. Reichs (Ed.), *Forensic Osteology: Advances in the Identification of Human Remains*, 2nd edn. Springfield, IL: Charles C. Thomas, pp. 63–85.

Burns, K. R., and Maples, W. R. (1976). Estimation of age from individual adult teeth. *Journal of Forensic Sciences* **21**: 343–356.

Byers, S., Akoshima, K., and Curran, B. (1989). Determination of adult stature from metatarsal length. *American Journal of Physical Anthropology* **79**: 275–279.

Calcagno, J. M. (1981). On the applicability of sexing human skeletal material by discriminant function analysis. *Journal of Human Evolution* **10**: 189–198.

Capasso, L., Kennedy, K. A. R., and Wilczak, C. A. (1999). *Atlas of Occupational Markers on Human Remains*. Teramo: Edigrafital S. p. A.

Catts, E. P., and Haskell, N. H. (1990). *Entomology and Death: A Procedural Guide*. Clemson, SC: Joyce's Print Shop.

Chakraborty, R., Shaw, M., and Schull, W. J. (1974). Exclusion of paternity: the current state of the art. *American Journal of Human Genetics* **26**: 477–488.

Chang, Y. M., Burgoyne, L. A., and Both, K. (2003). Higher failures of amelogenin sex test in an Indian population. *Journal of Forensic Sciences* **48**: 1309–1313.

Cho, H., Stout, S. D., Madsen, R. W., and Streeter, M. A. (2002). Population-specific histological age-estimating method: a model for known African-American and European-American skeletal remains. *Journal of Forensic Sciences* **47**: 12–18.

Christensen, A. M. (2004). The impact of *Daubert*: implications for testimony and research in forensic anthropology (and the use of frontal sinuses in personal identification). *Journal of Forensic Sciences* **49**: 427–430.

Christensen, A. M. (2005). Testing the reliability of frontal sinuses in positive identification. *Journal of Forensic Sciences* **50**: 18–22.

Christison, J. S. (1898). The medical and psychological aspects of the Luetgert case. Reprinted from *Chicago Law Journal* in J. S. Christison, *Crime and Criminals*, 2nd edn (1899). Chicago: S. T. Hurst, pp. 138–177.

Clegg, M., and Aiello, L. C. (1999). A comparison of the Nariokotome *Homo erectus* with juveniles from a modern human population. *American Journal of Physical Anthropology* **110**: 81–93.

Cox, M. (2000). Assessment of parturition. In Cox, M. and Mays, S. (Eds), *Human Osteology in Archaeology and Forensic Science*. London: Greenwich Medical Media, pp. 131–142.

Craig, E. A. (1995). Intercondylar shelf angle: a new method to determine race from the distal femur. *Journal of Forensic Sciences* **40**: 777–782.

Crist, T. A. J., Washburn, A., Park, H., Hood, I., and Hickey, M. A. (1997). Cranial bone displacement as a taphonomic process in potential child abuse cases. In W. D. Haglund and M. H. Sorg (Eds), *Forensic Taphonomy: The Postmortem Fate of Human Remains*. Boca Raton, FL: CRC Press, pp. 319–336.

Czuzak, M. H. (2005). Anthropological assessment of handedness. In *Encyclopedia of Forensic and Legal Medicine*. New York: Elsevier.

Davis, J. H. (1997). Preface. In W. D. Haglund and M. H. Sorg (Eds), *Forensic Taphonomy: The Postmortem Fate of Human Remains*. Boca Raton, FL: CRC Press, pp. xv-xvi.

Dawes, R. M., Faust, D., and Meehl, P. E. (1989). Clinical versus actuarial judgment. *Science* **243**: 1668–1674.

Demirjian, A., and Goldstein, H. (1976). New systems for dental maturity based on seven and four teeth. *Annals of Human Biology* **3**: 411–421.

Demirjian, A., Goldstein, H., and Tanner, J. M. (1973). A new system of dental age assessment. *Human Biology* **45**: 211–228.

DeVito, C., and Saunders, S. R. (1990). A discriminant function analysis of deciduous teeth to determine sex. *Journal of Forensic Sciences* **35**: 845–858.

Devriendt, W., Piercecchi-Marti, M-D., Adalian, P., Sanvoisin, A., Dutour, O., and Leonetti, G. (2005). Hyperostosis frontalis interna: forensic issues. *Journal of Forensic Sciences* **50**: 143–146.

DiBennardo, R., and Taylor, J. V. (1979). Sex assessment of the femur: a test of a new method. *American Journal of Physical Anthropology* **50**: 635–638.

DiBennardo, R., and Taylor, J. V. (1983). Multiple discriminant function analysis of sex and race in the postcranial skeleton. *American Journal of Physical Anthropology* **61**: 305–314.

DiMaio, V. J. M. (1985). *Gunshot Wounds: Practical Aspects of Firearms, Ballistics, and Forensic Techniques*. New York: Elsevier.

DiMaio, D. J., and DiMaio, V. J. M. (1993). *Forensic Pathology*. Boca Raton, FL: CRC Press.

Dixon, D. S. (1982). Keyhole lesions in gunshot wounds of the skull and direction of fire. *Journal of Forensic Sciences* **27**: 555–556.

Dorsey, G. A. (1896). The history of the study of anthropology at Harvard University. *Dennison Quarterly* **4**: 77–97.

Dudar, J. C., Pfeiffer, S., and Saunders, S. R. (1993). Evaluation of morphological and histological adult skeletal age-at-death estimation techniques using ribs. *Journal of Forensic Sciences* **38**: 677–685.

Dwight, T. (1905). The size of the articular surfaces of the long bones as characteristics of sex: an anthropological study. *American Journal of Anatomy* **4**: 19–32.

Edgar, H. J. H. (2005). Prediction of race using characteristics of dental morphology. *Journal of Forensic Sciences* **50**: 269–273.

Eveleth, P. B. (1975). Differences between ethnic groups in sex dimorphism of adult height. *Annals of Human Biology* **2**: 35–39.

Faigman, D. L. (2002). Is science different for lawyers? *Science* **297**: 339–340.

Falsetti, A. B. (1995). Sex assignment from metacarpals of the human hand. *Journal of Forensic Sciences* **40**: 774–776.

Fazekas, I. Gy., and Kósa, F. (1978). *Forensic Fetal Osteology*. Budapest: Akadémiai Kiadó.

Flecker, H. (1942). Time of appearance and fusion of ossification centers as observed by roentgenographic methods. *The American Journal of Roentgenology and Radium Therapy* **47**: 97–159.

Foster, K. R., Bernstein, D. E., and Huber, P. W. (1993). Science and the toxic tort. *Science* **261**: 1509, 1614.

France, D. L. (1998). Observational and metric analysis of sex in the skeleton. In K. J. Reichs (Ed.), *Forensic Osteology: Advances in the Identification of Human Remains*, 2nd edn. Springfield, IL: Charles C. Thomas, pp. 163–186.

Frutos, L. R. (2003). Brief communication: Sex determination accuracy of the minimum supero-inferior femoral neck diameter in a contemporary rural Guatemalan population. *American Journal of Physical Anthropology* **122**: 123–126.

Fully, G. (1956). Une nouvelle méthode de détermination de la taille. *Annales de Médicine Légale et de Criminologie* **36**: 266–273.

Fully, G., and Pineau, H. (1960). Détermination de la stature au moyen du squelette. *Annales de Médicine Légale et de Criminologie* **40**: 145–154.

Gaensslen, R. E., Bell, S. C., and Lee, H. C. (1987). Distributions of genetic markers in United States populations: II. Isozyme systems. *Journal of Forensic Sciences* **32**: 1348–1381.

Gaensslen, R. E., Berka, K. M., Pagliaro, E. M., Ruano, G., Messina, D., and Lee, H. C. (1994). Studies on DNA polymorphisms in human bone and soft tissues. *Analytica Chimica Acta* **288**: 3–16.

Galloway, A. (1988). Estimating actual height in the older individual. *Journal of Forensic Sciences* **33**: 126–136.

Galloway, A. (1997). The process of decomposition: a model from the Arizona-Sonoran desert. In W. D. Haglund and M. H. Sorg (Eds), *Forensic Taphomony: The Postmortem Fate of Human Remains*. Boca Raton, FL: CRC Press, pp. 139–150.

Galloway, A. (1999a). The circumstances of blunt force trauma. In A. Galloway (Ed.), *Broken Bones: Anthropological Analysis of Blunt Force Trauma.* Springfield, IL: Charles C. Thomas, pp. 224–254.

Galloway, A. (Ed.) (1999b). *Broken Bones: Anthropological Analysis of Blunt Force Trauma.* Springfield, IL: Charles C. Thomas.

Galloway, A., and Simmons, T. L. (1997). Education in forensic anthropology: appraisal and outlook. *Journal of Forensic Sciences* **42**: 796–801.

Galloway, A., Birkby, W. H., Kahana, T., and Fulginiti, L. (1990). Physical anthropology and the law: legal responsibilities of forensic anthropologists. *Yearbook of Physical Anthropology* **33**: 39–57.

Genoves, S. (1967). Proportionality of the long bones and their relation to stature among Mesoamericans. *American Journal of Physical Anthropology* **26**: 67–78.

Gilbert, R., and Gill, G. W. (1990). A metric technique for identifying American Indian femora. In G. W. Gill and S. Rhine (Eds), *Skeletal Attribution of Race.* Maxwell Museum of Anthropology Anthropological Papers No. 4. Albuquerque, NM: University of New Mexico Maxwell Museum of Anthropology, pp. 97–99.

Gilbert, B. M., and McKern, T. W. (1973). A method of aging the female *os pubis*. *American Journal of Physical Anthropology* **38**: 31–38.

Giles, E. (1964). Sex determination by discriminant function analysis of the mandible. *American Journal of Physical Anthropology* **22**: 129–135.

Giles, E. (1991). Corrections for age in estimating older adult's stature from long bones. *Journal of Forensic Sciences* **36**: 898–901.

Giles, E. (1993). Modifying stature estimation from the femur and tibia. *Journal of Forensic Sciences* **38**: 758–760.

Giles, E., and Elliot, O. (1962). Race identification from cranial measurements. *Journal of Forensic Sciences* **7**: 147–156.

Giles, E., and Elliot, O. (1963). Sex determination by discriminant function analysis of crania. *American Journal of Physical Anthropology* **21**: 53–68.

Giles, E., and Hutchinson, D. L. (1991). Stature- and age-related bias in self-reported stature. *Journal of Forensic Sciences* **36**: 765–780.

Giles, E., and Klepinger, L. L. (1988). Confidence intervals for estimates based on linear regression in forensic anthropology. *Journal of Forensic Sciences* **33**: 1218–1222.

Giles, E., and Klepinger, L. L. (1999). The butcher who rendered his wife? Chicago's Luetgert case and the beginning of American forensic anthropology. *Proceedings of the American Academy of Forensic Sciences* **5**: 295–296 (abstract).

Giles, E., and Vallandigham, P. H. (1991). Height estimation from foot and shoeprint length. *Journal of Forensic Sciences* **36**: 1134–1151.

Gill, G. W. (1998). Craniofacial criteria in the skeletal attribution of race. In K. J. Reichs (Ed.), *Forensic Osteology: Advances in the Identification of Human Remains.* Springfield, IL: Charles C. Thomas, pp. 293–317.

Gill, G. W., and Rhine, S. (Eds) (1990). *Skeletal Attribution of Race.* Maxwell Museum of Anthropology Anthropological Papers No. 4. Albuquerque, NM: University of New Mexico Maxwell Museum of Anthropology.

Gill, G. W., Hughes, S. S., Bennett, S. M., and Gilbert, B. M. (1988). Racial identification from the midfacial skeleton with special reference to American Indians and whites. *Journal of Forensic Sciences* **33**: 92–99.

Gill-King, H. (1997). Chemical and ultrastructural aspects of decomposition. In W. D. Haglund and M. H. Sorg (Eds), *Forensic Taphonomy: The Postmortem Fate of Human Remains.* Boca Raton, FL: CRC Press, pp. 93–108.

Glassman, D. M., and Bass, W. M. (1986). Bilateral asymmetry of long arm bones and jugular foramen: implications for handedness. *Journal of Forensic Sciences* **31**: 589–595.

Goff, M. L., Brown, W. A., Kamani, A. H., and Omori, A. I. (1991). Effect of heroine in decomposing tissues on the development rate of *Boettcherisca pergrina* (Diptera, Sarcophagidae) and implications of this effect on estimation of postmortem internals using arthropod development patterns. *Journal of Forensic Sciences* **36**: 537–542.

Gold, J. A., Zaremski, M. J., Lev, E. R., and Shefren, D. H. (1993). Daubert v Merrell Dow: the Supreme Court tackles scientific evidence in the courtroom. *Journal of the American Medical Association* **270**: 2964–2967.

Gordon, C. C., and Buikstra, J. E. (1992). Linear models for the prediction of stature from foot and boot dimensions. *Journal of Forensic Sciences* **37**: 771–782.

Grunbaum, B. W., Selvin, S., Pace, N., and Black, D. M. (1978). Frequency distribution and discrimination probability of twelve protein genetic variants in human blood as functions of race, sex, and age. *Journal of Forensic Sciences* **23**: 577–587.

Gülekon, I. N., and Turgut, H. B. (2003). The external occipital protuberance: can it be used as a criterion in the determination of sex? *Journal of Forensic Sciences* **48**: 513–516.

Gustafson, G. (1950). Age determinations on teeth. *Journal of the American Dental Association* **41**: 45–54.

Haglund, W. D. (1997). Dogs and coyotes: postmortem involvement with human remains. In W. D. Haglund and M. H. Sorg (Eds), *Forensic Taphonomy: The Postmortem Fate of Human Remains.* Boca Raton, FL: CRC Press, pp. 367–381.

Haglund, W. D., and Sorg, M. H. (Eds) (1997). *Forensic Taphonomy: The Postmortem Fate of Human Remains.* Boca Raton, FL: CRC Press.

Haglund, W. D., Reay, D. T., and Swindler, D. R. (1989). Canid scavenging/ disarticulation sequence of human remains in the Pacific Northwest. *Journal of Forensic Sciences* **34**: 587–606.

Haglund, W. D., and Sorg, M. H. (Eds) (2002a). *Advances in Forensic Taphonomy: Method, Theory, and Archaeological Perspectives.* Boca Raton, FL: CRC Press.

Haglund, W. D., and Sorg, M. H. (2002b). Human remains in water environments. In W. D. Haglund and M. H. Sorg (Eds), *Advances in Forensic Taphonomy:*

Method, Theory, and Archaeological Perspectives. Boca Raton, FL: CRC Press, pp. 202–218.

Hansen, M. (2000). Expertise to go. *American Bar Association Journal*, February 2000, pp. 44–52.

Harris, E. F., Hicks, J. D., and Barcroft, B. D. (2001). Tissue contributions to sex and race: differences in tooth crown size of deciduous molars. *American Journal of Physical Anthropology* **115**: 223–237.

Harris, E. F., and McKee, J. H. (1990). Tooth mineralization standards for blacks and whites from the middle southern United States. *Journal of Forensic Sciences* **35**: 859–872.

Harris, E. F., and Rathbun, T. A. (1991). Ethnic differences in the apportionment of tooth sizes. In M. A. Kelley and C. S. Larsen (Eds), *Advances in Dental Anthropology.* New York: Alan R. Liss, pp. 121–142.

Harruff, R. C. (1995). Comparison of contact shotgun wounds of the head produced by different gauge shotguns. *Journal of Forensic Sciences* **40**: 801–804.

Harvey, M., and King, M.-C. (2002). The use of DNA in the identification of post-mortem remains. In W. D. Haglund and M. H. Sorg (Eds), *Advances in Forensic Taphonomy: Method, Theory, and Archaeological Perspectives.* Boca Raton, FL: CRC Press, pp. 473–486.

Haskell, N. H., Hall, R. D., Cervenka, V. J., and Clark, M. A. (1997). On the body: insects' life stage presence, their postmortem artifacts. In W. D. Haglund and M. H. Sorg (Eds), *Forensic Taphonomy: The Postmortem Fate of Human Remains.* Boca Raton, FL: CRC Press, pp. 415–448.

Hawkey, D. E. (1998). Disability, compassion and the skeletal record: using musculoskeletal stress markers (MSM) to construct an osteobiography from early New Mexico. *International Journal of Osteoarchaeology* **8**: 326–340.

Hawkey, D. E., and Merbs, C. F. (1995). Activity-induced musculoskeletal stress markers (MSM) and subsistence strategy changes among ancient Hudson Bay Eskimos. *International Journal of Osteoarchaeology* **5**: 324–338.

Hegler, R. (1984). Burned remains. In T. A. Rathbun and J. E. Buikstra (Eds), *Human Identification: Case Studies in Forensic Anthropology.* Springfield, IL: Charles C. Thomas, pp. 148–158.

Helfer, R. E., and Kempe, R. S. (1987). *The Battered Child.* Chicago, IL: University of Chicago Press.

Helfer, R. E., Slovis, T. L., and Black, M. (1977). Injuries resulting when small children fall out of bed. *Pediatrics* **60**: 533–535.

Herrman, N. P., and Bennett, J. L. (1999). The differentiation of traumatic and heat-related fracture in burned bone. *Journal of Forensic Sciences* **44**: 461–469.

Hertzog, K. P., Garn, S. M., and Hempy, H. O. III (1969). Partitioning the effects of secular trend and aging on adult stature. *Journal of Physical Anthropology* **31**: 111–115.

Hillson, S. (1986). *Teeth.* New York: Cambridge University Press.

Hillson, S. (1996). *Dental Anthropology.* Cambridge: Cambridge University Press.

Hobbs, C. J. (1984). Skull fracture and the diagnosis of abuse. *Archives of Disease in Childhood* **59**: 246–252.

Hoffman, J. M. (1979). Age estimations from diaphyseal lengths: two months to twelve years. *Journal of Forensic Sciences* **24**: 461–469.

Hoffman, J. M. (1984). Identification of nonskeletonized bear paws and human feet. In T. A. Rathbun and J. E. Buikstra (Eds), *Human Identification: Case Studies in Forensic Anthropology.* Springfield, IL: Charles C. Thomas, pp. 96–106.

Hoffrage, U., Lindsey, S., Hertwig, R., and Gigerenzer, G. (2000). Communicating statistical information. *Science* **290**: 2261–2262.

Holland, T. D. (1986). Sex determination of fragmentary crania by analysis of the cranial base. *American Journal of Physical Anthropology* **70**: 203–208.

Holland, T. D. (1989). Use of the cranial base in the identification of fire victims. *Journal of Forensic Sciences* **34**: 458–460.

Holland, T. D. (1991). Sex assessment using the proximal tibia. *American Journal of Physical Anthropology* **85**: 221–227.

Holland, T. D. (1992). Estimation of adult stature from fragmentary tibias. *Journal of Forensic Sciences* **37**: 1223–1229.

Hollien, H. (1990). The expert witness: ethics and responsibilities. *Journal of Forensic Sciences* **35**: 1414–1423.

Hooton, E. A. (1943). Medico-legal aspects of physical anthropology. *Clinics* **1**: 1612–1624.

Houck, M. H. (1998). Skeletal trauma and the individualization of knife marks in bone. In K. J. Reichs (Ed.), *Forensic Osteology: Advances in the Identification of Human Remains*, 2nd edn. Springfield, IL: Charles C. Thomas, pp. 410–424.

Houghton, P. (1977). Rocker jaws. *American Journal of Physical Anthropology* **47**: 365–370.

Huber, P. W. (1991). *Galileo's Revenge: Junk Science in the Courtroom.* New York: Basic Books.

Humphrey, J. H., and Hutchinson, D. L. (2001). Macroscopic characteristics of hacking trauma. *Journal of Forensic Sciences* **46**: 228–233.

Humphrey, L. (2000). Growth studies of past populations: an overview and an example. In M. Cox and S. Mays (Eds), *Human Osteology in Archaeology and Forensic Science.* London: Greenwich Medical Media, pp. 23–38.

Hunt, D. R. (1990). Sex determination in the subadult ilia: an indirect test of Weaver's nonmetric sexing method. *Journal of Forensic Sciences* **35**: 881–885.

İşcan, M. Y., and Loth, S. R. (1986). Estimation of age and determination of sex from the sternal rib. In K. J. Reichs (Ed.), *Forensic Osteology: Advances in the Identification of Human Remains.* Springfield, IL: Charles C. Thomas, pp. 68–89.

İşcan, M. Y., and Miller-Shaivitz, P. (1984a). Determination of sex from the tibia. *American Journal of Physical Anthropology* **64**: 53–57.

İşcan, M. Y., and Miller-Shaivitz, P. (1984b). Discriminant function sexing of the tibia. *Journal of Forensic Sciences* **29**: 1087–1093.

İşcan, M. Y., Loth, S. R., and Wright, R. K. (1984). Age estimation from the rib by phase analysis: white males. *Journal of Forensic Sciences* **29**: 1094–1104.

İşcan, M. Y., Loth, S. R., and Wright, R. K. (1985). Age estimation from the rib by phase analysis: white females. *Journal of Forensic Sciences* **30**: 853–863.

İşcan, M. Y., Loth, S. R., and Wright, R. K. (1987). Racial variation in the sternal extremity of the rib and its effect on age determination. *Journal of Forensic Sciences* **32**: 452–466.

İşcan, M. Y., Loth, S. R., and Wright, R. K. (1993). Casts of age phases from the sternal end of the rib for white males and females. Bellvue, CO: France Casting.

Jantz, R. L. (1992). Modification of the Trotter and Gleser female stature estimation formulae. *Journal of Forensic Sciences* **37**: 1230–1235.

Jantz, R. L. (1993). Author's response. *Journal of Forensic Sciences* **38**: 760–763.

Jantz, R. L., Hunt, D. R., and Meadows, L. (1995). The measure and mismeasure of the tibia: implications for stature estimation. *Journal of Forensic Sciences* **40**: 758–761.

Jit, I., Jhingan, V., and Kulkarni, M. (1980). Sexing the human sternum. *American Journal of Physical Anthropology* **53**: 217–224.

Joyce, C., and Stover, E. (1991). *Witnesses from the Grave.* Boston: Little, Brown.

Katz, D., and Suchey, J. M. (1986). Age determination of the male os pubis. *American Journal of Physical Anthropology* **69**: 427–435.

Katz, D., and Suchey, J. M. (1989). Race differences in pubic symphyseal aging patterns in the male. *American Journal of Physical Anthropology* **80**: 167–172.

Kaye, D. H., and Sensabaugh, G. F. (2000). Reference guide on DNA evidence. In Federal Judicial Center 2000 (Ed.), *Reference Manual on Scientific Evidence*, 2nd edn. New York: Lexis, pp. 485–576.

Kelley, M. A. (1979). Parturition and pelvic changes. *American Journal of Physical Anthropology* **51**: 541–546.

Kennedy, K. A. R. (1989). Skeletal markers of occupational stress. In M. Y. İşcan and K. A. R. Kennedy (Eds), *Reconstruction of Life From the Skeleton.* New York: Alan R. Liss, pp. 129–160.

Kennedy, K. A. R. (1995). But, professor, why teach race identification if races don't exist? *Journal of Forensic Sciences* **40**: 797–800.

Kerley, E. R. (1965). The microscopic determination of age in human bones. *American Journal of Physical Anthropology* **23**: 149–163.

Kerley, E. R. (1970). Estimation of skeletal age: after about age 30. In T. D. Stewart (Ed.), *Personal Identification in Mass Disasters.* Washington, DC: Smithsonian Institution, pp. 57–70.

Kerley, E. R. (1973). Forensic anthropology. In C. H. Wecht (Ed.), *Legal Medicine Annual.* New York: Appleton-Century-Crofts, pp. 163–198.

Kerley, E. R. (1976). Forensic anthropology and crimes involving children. *Journal of Forensic Sciences* **21**: 333–339.

Kerley, E. R. (1978). The identification of battered-infant skeletons. *Journal of Forensic Sciences* **23**: 163–168.

Kerley, E. R., and Ubelaker, D. H. (1978). Revisions in the microscopic method of estimating age at death in human cortical bone. *American Journal of Physical Anthropology* **49**: 545–546.

Key, C. A., Aiello, L. C., and Molleson, T. (1994). Cranial suture closure and its implications for age estimation. *International Journal of Osteoarchaeology* **4**: 193–207.

King, M.-C., and Motulsky, A. G. (2002). Mapping human history. *Science* **298**: 2342–2343.

Kipling, D., Davis, T., Ostler, E. L., and Faragher, R. G. A. (2004). What can progeroid syndromes tell us about human aging? *Science* **305**: 1426–1431.

Kirk, N. J., Wood, R. E., and Goldstein, M. (2002). Skeletal identification using the frontal sinus region: a retrospective study of 39 cases. *Journal of Forensic Sciences* **47**: 318–323.

Kirkham, W. R., Andrews, E. E., Snow, C.C., Grape, P. M., and Snyder, L. (1977). Postmortem pink teeth. *Journal of Forensic Sciences* **22**: 119–131.

Kleinman, P. K., Marks, S. C. Jr., Richmond, J. M., and Blackbourne, B. D. (1995). Inflicted skeletal injury: a postmortem radiologic-histopathological study in 31 infants. *American Journal of Roentgenology* **165**: 647–650.

Klepinger, L. L. (1978). The effect of severe bedsores on bone and its forensic implications. *Journal of Forensic Sciences* **23**:754–757.

Klepinger, L. L. (1999). Unusual skeletal anomalies and pathologies in forensic casework. In S. I. Fairgrieve (Ed.), *Forensic Osteological Analysis: A Book of Case Studies.* Springfield, IL: Charles C. Thomas, pp. 226–236.

Klepinger, L. L. (2001). Stature, maturation variation and secular trends in forensic anthropology. *Journal of Forensic Sciences* **46**: 788–790.

Klepinger, L., and Giles, E. (1998). Clarification or confusion: statistical interpretation in forensic anthropology. In K. J. Reichs (Ed.), *Forensic Osteology: Advances in the Identification of Human Remains*, 2nd edn. Springfield, IL: Charles C. Thomas, pp. 427–440.

Klepinger, L. L., and Heidingsfelder, J. A. (1996). Probable torticollis revealed in decapitated skull. *Journal of Forensic Sciences* **41**: 693–696.

Klepinger, L., and Wisseman, S. (2002). Characterization of archaeological skeletal material using PIMA (portable infrared mineral analyzer). In *33rd International Symposium in Archaeometry*, Amsterdam, Program and Abstracts, pp. 174–175.

Klepinger, L. L., Katz, S., Micozzi, M. S., and Carroll, L. (1992). Evaluation of cast methods for estimating age from the os pubis. *Journal of Forensic Sciences* **37**: 763–770.

Krantz, G. S. (1968). A new method of counting mammal bones. *American Journal of Archaeology* **72**: 286–288.

Krogman, W. M. (1939). A guide to the identification of human skeletal material. *FBI Law Enforcement Bulletin* **8**: 3–31.

Krogman, W. M. (1962). *The Human Skeleton in Forensic Medicine.* Springfield, IL: Charles C. Thomas.

Krogman, W. M., and İşcan, M. Y. (1986). *Human The Skeleton in Forensic Medicine*, 2nd edn. Springfield, IL: Charles C. Thomas.

Kuehn, C. M., Taylor, K. M., Mann, F.A., Wilson, A. J., and Harruff, R. C. (2002). Validation of chest X-ray comparisons for unknown decedent identification. *Journal of Forensic Sciences* **47**: 725–729.

Lamendin, H., Baccino, E., Humbert, J. F., Taverier, J. C., Nossintchouk, R. M., and Zerilli, A. (1992). A simple technique for age estimation in adult corpses: The two criteria dental method. *Journal of Forensic Sciences* **37**: 1373–1379.

Lease, L. R., and Sciulli, P. W. (2005). Brief communication: Discrimination between European-American and African-American children based on deciduous dental metrics and morphology. *American Journal of Physical Anthropology* **126**: 56–60.

Leventhal, J. M., Thomas, S. A., Rosenfield, N. S., and Markovitz, R. I. (1993). Fractures in young children. Distinguishing child abuse from unintentional injuries. *American Journal of Diseases of Children* **147**: 87–92.

Lincoln, F. C. (1930). Calculating waterfowl abundance on the basis of banding returns. *United States Department of Agriculture Circular* **118**: 1–4.

Loerzel, R. (2003). *Alchemy of Bones: Chicago's Luetgert Murder Case of 1897.* Urbana, IL: University of Illinois Press.

Loth, S. R., and Henneberg, M. (2001). Sexually dimorphic mandibular morphology in the first few years of life. *American Journal of Physical Anthropology* **115**: 179–186.

Loth, S. R., and İşcan, M. Y. (1989). Morphological assessment of age in the adult: the thoracic region. In M. Y. İşcan (Ed.), *Age Markers in the Human Skeleton.* Springfield, IL: Charles C. Thomas, pp. 105–135.

Lovejoy, C. O., Meindl, R. S., Mensforth, R. P., and Barton, T. J. (1985a). Multifactorial determination of skeletal age at death: a method and blind tests of its accuracy. *American Journal of Physical Anthropology* **68**: 1–14.

Lovejoy, C. O., Meindl, R. S., Pryzbeck, T. R., and Mensforth, R. P. (1985b). Chronological metamorphosis of the auricular surface of the ilium: a new method for the determination of adult skeletal age at death. *American Journal of Physical Anthropology* **68**: 15–28.

Lovell, N. C. (1989). Test of Phenice's technique for determining sex from the os pubis. *American Journal of Physical Anthropology* **79**: 117–120.

Lubet, S. (1998). *Expert Testimony: A Guide for Expert Witnesses and the Lawyers Who Examine Them.* Notre Dame, IN: National Institute for Trial Advocacy.

Lundy, J. K. (1988). A report on the use of Fully's anatomical method to estimate stature in military skeletal remains. *Journal of Forensic Sciences* **33**: 534–539.

MacHovel, F. J. (1987). *The Expert Witness Survival Manual.* Springfield, IL: Charles C. Thomas.

Mann, R. W., Bass, W. M., and Meadows, L. (1990). Time since death and decomposition of the human body: variables and observations in case and experimental field studies. *Journal of Forensic Sciences* **35**: 103–111.

Maples, W. R. (1986). Trauma analysis by the forensic anthropologist. In K. J. Reichs (Ed.), *Forensic Osteology: Advances in the Identification of Human Remains.* Springfield, IL: Charles C. Thomas, pp. 218–228.

Maples, W. R., and Browning, M. (1994). *Dead Men Do Tell Tales.* New York: Doubleday.

Maples, W. R., and Rice, P. M. (1979). Some difficulties in the Gustafson dental age estimations. *Journal of Forensic Sciences* **24**: 168–172.

Maresh, M. M. (1955). Linear growth of long bones of extremities from infancy to adolescence. *American Journal of Diseases of Children.* **89**: 725–742.

Masset, C. (1989). Age estimates on the basis of cranial sutures. In M. Y. İşcan (Ed.), *Age Markers in the Human Skeleton.* Springfield, IL: Charles C. Thomas.

Mayne Correia, P. M. (1997). Fire modification of bone: a review of the literature. In W. D. Haglund and M. H. Sorg (Eds), *Forensic Taphonomy: The Postmortem Fate of Human Remains.* Boca Raton, FL: CRC Press, pp. 275–293.

McKern, T. W., and Stewart, T. D. (1957). *Skeletal Age Changes in Young American Males.* Quartermaster Research and Development Center, Environment Protection Research Division, Technical Report EP-45. Natick, MA: Headquarters Quartermaster Research and Development Command.

Meadows, L., and Jantz, R. L. (1992). Estimation of stature from metacarpal lengths. *Journal of Forensic Sciences* **37**: 147–154.

Meadows, L., and Jantz, R. L. (1995). Allometric secular change in long bones from the 1800s to the present. *Journal of Forensic Sciences* **40**: 762–767.

Meindl, R. S., and Lovejoy, C. O. (1985). Ectocranial suture closure: a revised method for the determination of skeletal age at death based on the lateral–anterior sutures. *American Journal of Physical Anthropology* **68**: 57–66.

Meindl, R. S., and Lovejoy, C. O. (1989). Age changes in the pelvis: implications for paleodemography. In M. Y. İşcan (Ed.), *Age Markers in the Human Skeleton.* Springfield, IL: Charles C. Thomas.

Meindl, R. S., Lovejoy, C.O., Mensforth, R. P., and Don Carlos, L. (1985a). Accuracy and direction of error in the sexing of the skeleton: Implications for paleodemography. *American Journal of Physical Anthropology* **68**: 79–85.

Meindl, R. S., Lovejoy, C. O., Mensforth, R. P., and Walker, R. A. (1985b). A revised method of age determination using the os pubis with a review and tests of accuracy of other current methods of pubic symphyseal aging. *American Journal of Physical Anthropology* **68**: 29–45.

Merbs, C. F. (1996). Spondololysis and spondololisthesis: a cost of being erect and biped or a clever adaptation? *Yearbook of Physical Anthropology* **39**: 201–220.

Mervis, J. (1993). Supreme court to judges: start thinking like scientists. *Science* **261**: 22.

Meservy, C. J., Towbin, R., McLauren, R. L., Myers, P. A., and Ball, W. (1987). Radiographic characteristics of skull fractures resulting from child abuse. *American Journal of Roentgenology* **149**: 173–175.

Micozzi, M. S. (1991). *Postmortem Change in Human and Animal Remains: A Systematic Approach.* Springfield, IL: Charles C. Thomas.

Mittler, D. M., and Sheridan, S. G. (1992). Sex determination in subadults using auricular surface morphology: a forensic science perspective. *Journal of Forensic Sciences* **37**: 1068–1075.

Moenssens, A. A., Starrs, J. E., Henderson, C. E., and Inbau, F. E. (1995). *Scientific Evidence in Criminal and Civil Cases*, 4th edn. Westbury, NY: The Foundation Press.

Molleson, T., and Cox, M. (1993). *The Spitalfields Project: The Middling Sort, Vol. 2: The Anthropology.* CBA Research Report 86. Walmgate, York: Council for British Archaeology.

Moorrees, C. F. A., Fanning, E. A., and Hunt, E. E. Jr (1963a). Formation and resorption of three deciduous teeth in children. *American Journal of Physical Anthropology* **21**: 205–213.

Moorrees, C. F. A., Fanning, E. A., and Hunt, E. E. Jr (1963b). Age variation of formation stages for ten permanent teeth. *Journal of Dental Research* **42**: 1490–1502.

Mourant, A. E., Kopéc, A. C., and Domaniewska-Sobcak, K. (1976). *The Distribution of the Human Blood Groups and Other Polymorphisms*, 2nd edn. New York: Oxford University Press.

Murad, T. A. (1998). The growing popularity of cremation versus inhumation. In K. J. Reichs (Ed.), *Forensic Osteology: Advances in the Identification of Human Remains*, 2nd edn. Springfield, IL: Charles C. Thomas, pp. 86–105.

Murphy, W. A., and Gantner, G. E. (1982). Radiologic examination of anatomic parts and skeletonized remains. *Journal of Forensic Sciences* **27**: 9–18.

Murray, K. A., and Murray, T. (1991). A test of the auricular surface aging technique. *Journal of Forensic Sciences* **36**: 1162–1169.

Nawrocki, S. P. (1998). Regression formulae for estimating age at death from cranial suture closure. In K. J. Reichs (Ed.), *Forensic Osteology: Advances in Identification of Human Remains*, 2nd edn. Springfield, IL: Charles C. Thomas, pp. 276–292.

Nelson, R. (1992). A microscopic comparison of fresh and burned bone. *Journal of Forensic Sciences* **37**: 1055–1060.

O'Halloran, R. L., and Lundy, J. K. (1987). Age and ossification of the hyoid bone: forensic implications. *Journal of Forensic Sciences* **32**: 1655–1659.

Ortner, D. J., and Putschar, W. G. J. (1985). *Identification of Pathological Conditions in Human Skeletal Remains.* Washington, DC: Smithsonian Institution Press.

Osbourne, D. L., Simmons, T. L., and Nawrocki, S. P. (2004). Reconsidering the auricular surface as an indicator of age at death. *Journal of Forensic Sciences* **49**: 905–911.

Ousley, S. (1995). Should we estimate biological or forensic stature? *Journal of Forensic Sciences* **40**: 768–773.

Ousley, S., and Jantz, R. L. (1998). The forensic data bank: documenting skeletal trends in the United States. In K. J. Reichs (Ed.), *Forensic Osteology: Advances in the Identification of Human Remains*, 2nd edn. Springfield, IL: Charles C. Thomas, pp. 441–458.

Parsons, T. J., and Weedn, V. W. (1997). Preservation and recovery of DNA in postmortem specimens and trace samples. In W. D. Haglund and M. H. Sorg (Eds), *Forensic Taphonomy: The Postmortem Fate of Human Remains.* Boca Raton, FL: CRC Press, pp. 109–138.

Pfeiffer, S., Milne, S., and Stevenson, R. M. (1998). The natural decomposition of adipocere. *Journal of Forensic Sciences* **43**: 368–370.

Phenice, T. W. (1969). A newly developed visual method of sexing the os pubis. *American Journal of Physical Anthropology* **30**: 297–301.

Pollanen, M. S., and Chiasson, D. A. (1996). Fracture of the hyoid bone in strangulation: comparison of fractured and unfractured hyoids from victims of strangulation. *Journal of Forensic Sciences* **41**: 110–113.

Prince, D. A., and Ubelaker, D. H. (2002). Application of Lamendin's adult dental aging technique to a diverse skeletal sample. *Journal of Forensic Sciences* **47**: 107–116.

Pope, E. J., and Smith, O. C. (2004). Identification of traumatic injury in burned cranial bone: an experimental approach. *Journal of Forensic Sciences* **49**: 431–440.

Quatrehomme, G., Bolla, M., Muller, M., Rocca, J.-P., Grévin, G., Bailet, P., and Ollier, A. (1998). Experimental single controlled study of burned bones: contribution of scanning electron microscopy. *Journal of Forensic Sciences* **43**: 417–422.

Reichs, K. J. (1998). Postmortem dismemberment: recovery, analysis, and interpretation. In K. J. Reichs (Ed.), *Forensic Osteology: Advances in the Identification of Human Remains*, 2nd edn. Springfield, IL: Charles C. Thomas, pp. 353–388.

Rhine, J. S., and Curran, B. K. (1990). Multiple gunshot wounds to the head: an anthropological view. *Journal of Forensic Sciences* **35**: 1236–1245.

Rhine, S. (1990). Non-metric skull racing. In G. W. Gill and S. Rhine (Eds), *Skeletal Attribution of Race*. Maxwell Museum of Anthropology Anthropological Papers No. 4. Albuquerque, NM: University of New Mexico Maxwell Museum of Anthropology, pp. 9–20.

Rhine, S. (1998) *Bone Voyage: A Journey in Forensic Anthropology.* Albuquerque, NM: University of New Mexico Press.

Ridlon, J. (1899). Minutes of the Medico-Legal Society of Chicago. *Chicago Medical Recorder* **16**: 172–179.

Robbins, L. M. (1985). *Footprints: Collection, Analysis, and Interpretation.* Springfield, IL: Charles C. Thomas.

Robbins, L. M. (1986). Estimating height and weight from size of footprints. *Journal of Forensic Sciences* **31**: 79–98.

Rodolph, D., Scheithauer, R., and Pollak, S. (1995). Postmortem injuries inflicted by the domestic golden hamster: morphological aspects and evidence of DNA typing. *Forensic Science International* **72**: 81–90.

Rodriguez, W. C. III, and Bass, W. M. (1985). Decomposition of buried bodies and methods that may aid in their location. *Journal of Forensic Sciences* **30**: 836–852.

Rogers, T. L. (1999). A visual method of determining the sex of skeletal remains using the distal humerus. *Journal of Forensic Sciences* **44**: 57–60.

Romer, A. S. (1949). *The Vertebrate Body.* Philadelphia, PA: W. B. Saunders.

Rosenberg, N. A., Pritchard, J. K., Weber, J. L., Cann, H. M., Kidd, K. K., Zhivotovsky, L. A., and Feldman, M. W. (2002). Genetic structure of human populations. *Science* **298**: 2381–2385.

Rösing, F. W. (1983). Sexing immature human skeletons. *Journal of Human Evolution* **12**: 149–155.

Rossi, F. F. (1991). *Expert Witness.* Chicago, IL: Section of Litigation, American Bar Association.

Rothschild, M. A., and Schneider, V. (1997). On the temporal onset of postmortem animal scavenging "motivation" of the animal. *Forensic Science International* **89**: 57–64.

Sauer, N. J. (1998). The timing of injuries and manner of death: distinguishing among antemortem, perimortem and postmortem trauma. In K. J. Reichs (Ed.), *Forensic Osteology: Advances in the Identification of Human Remains*, 2nd edn. Springfield, IL: Charles C. Thomas, pp. 321–332.

Sauer, N. J., Brantley, R. E., and Barondess, D. A. (1988). The effects of aging on the comparability of antemortem and postmortem radiographs. *Journal of Forensic Sciences* **33**: 1223–1230.

Saul, J. M., and Saul, F. P. (1999). Biker's bones: an avocational syndrome. In S. I. Fairgrieve (Ed.), *Forensic Osteological Analysis: A Book of Case Studies.* Springfield, IL: Charles C. Thomas, pp. 237–250.

Saunders, S. R. (1992). Subadult skeletons and growth related studies. In S. R. Saunders and M. A. Katzenberg (Eds), *Skeletal Biology of Past Peoples: Research Methods.* New York: Wiley-Liss, pp. 1–20.

Scheuer, J. L., and Elkington, N. M. (1993). Sex determination from metacarpals and the first proximal phalanx. *Journal of Forensic Sciences* **38**: 769–778.

Scheuer, L. (2002). Brief communication: A blind test of mandibular morphology for sexing mandibles in the first few years of life. *American Journal of Physical Anthropology* **119**: 189–191.

Scheuer, L., and Black, S. (2000). *Developmental Juvenile Osteology.* San Diego, CA: Academic Press.

Schmitt, A. (2004). Age-at-death assessment using the os pubis and auricular surface of the ilium: a test on an identified Asian sample. *International Journal of Osteoarchaeology* **14**: 1–6.

Schour, I., and Massler, M. (1941). The development of the human dentition. *The Journal of the American Dental Association* **28**: 1153–1160.

Schulter-Ellis, F. P. (1980). Evidence of handedness on documented skeletons. *Journal of Forensic Sciences* **25**: 624–630.

Schutkowski, H. (1987). Sex determination of fetal and neonate skeletons by means of discriminant analysis. *International Journal of Anthropology* **2**: 347–352.

Schutkowski, H. (1993). Sex determination in infant and juvenile skeletons using morphological features in mandible and ilium. *American Journal of Physical Anthropology* **90**: 199–205.

Schwarzer, W. W., and Cecil, J. S. (2000). Management of expert evidence. In Federal Judicial Center 2000 (Eds), *Reference Manual on Scientific Evidence*, 2nd edn. New York: Lexis Publishing, pp. 39–66.

Sciulli, P. W., and Giesen, M. J. (1993). Brief communication: An update on stature estimation in prehistoric Native Americans of Ohio. *American Journal of Physical Anthropology* **92**: 395–399.

Seber, G. A. F. (1982). *The Estimation of Animal Abundance and Related Parameters.* London: Charles Griffen.

Shipman, P., Foster, G., and Schoeninger, M. (1984). Burnt bones and teeth: an experimental study of color, morphology, crystal structure, and shrinkage. *Journal of Archaeological Science* **11**: 307–325.

Simmons, T., Jantz, R. L., and Bass, W. M. (1990). Stature estimation from fragmentary femora: a revision of the Steele method. *Journal of Forensic Sciences* **35**: 628–636.

Šlaus, M., Strinovic′, D., Škavic′, J., and Petrovečki, V. (2003). Discriminant function sexing of fragmentary and complete femora: standards for contemporary Croatia. *Journal of Forensic Sciences* **48**: 509–512.

Smith, B. H. (1991). Standards of human tooth formation and dental age assessment. In M. A. Kelly and C. S. Larsen (Eds), *Advances in Dental Anthropology.* New York: Wiley-Liss, pp. 143–168.

Smith, S. L. (1996). Attribution of hand bones to sex and population groups. *Journal of Forensic Sciences* **41**: 469–477.

Smith, S. L. (2004). Skeletal age, dental age, and the maturation of KMN-WT 15000. *American Journal of Physical Anthropology* **125**: 105–120.

Snow, C. C. (1982). Forensic anthropology. *Annual Review of Anthropology* **34**: 97–131.

Snow, C. C., Hartman, S., Giles, E., and Young, F. A. (1979). Sex and race determination of crania by calipers and computer: a test of Giles and Elliot discrimnant functions in 52 forensic science cases. *Journal of Forensic Sciences* **24**: 448–460.

Sorg, M. H., Andrews, R.P., İşcan, M. Y. (1989). Radiographic aging of the adult. In M. Y. İşcan (Ed.), *Age Markers in the Human Skeleton.* Springfield, IL: Charles C. Thomas, pp. 169–193.

Spencer, F. (1997). Dorsey, George Amos (1868–1931). In F. Spencer (Ed.), *History of Physical Anthropology: An Encyclopedia.* New York: Garland, pp. 352–353.

Starrs, J. E. (2002). Suing expert witnesses: two courts go cattywampus on absolute immunity. *Academy News: American Academy of Forensic Sciences* **32**: 15–17.

Steadman, D. W., and Haglund, W. D. (2005). The scope of anthropological contributions to human rights investigations. *Journal of Forensic Sciences* **50**: 23–30.

Steele, D. G. (1970). Estimation of stature from fragments of long limb bones. In T. D. Stewart (Ed.), *Personal Identification in Mass Disasters.* Washington, DC: Smithsonian Institution Press, pp. 85–97.

Steele, D. G. (1976). The estimation of sex on the basis of the talus and calcaneus. *American Journal of Physical Anthropology* **45**: 581–588.

Steele, D. G., and Bramblett, C. A. (1988). *The Anatomy and Biology of the Human Skeleton.* College Station, TX: Texas A&M University Press.

Stevenson, P. H. (1924). Age order of epiphyseal union in man. *American Journal of Physical Anthropology* **7**: 53–93.

Stewart, T. D. (1962). Anterior femoral curvature: its utility for race identification. *Human Biology* **34**: 49–62.

Stewart, T. D. (1970). Identification of the scars of parturition in the skeletal remains of females. In T. D. Stewart (Ed.), *Personal Identification in Mass Disasters.* Washington, DC: Smithsonian Institution Press, pp. 127–135.

Stewart, T. D. (1979a). *Essentials of Forensic Anthropology.* Springfield, IL: Charles C. Thomas.

Stewart, T. D. (1979b). A tribute to the French forensic anthropologist Georges Fully (1926–1973). *Journal of Forensic Sciences* **24**: 916–924.

Stirland, A. J. (1998). Musculoskeletal evidence for activity: problems of evaluation. *International Journal of Osteoarchaeology* **8**: 354–362.

Stout, S. D. (1986). The use of bone histomorphology in skeletal identification: the case of Francisco Pizarro. *Journal of Forensic Sciences* **31**: 296–300.

Stout, S. D. (1989). The use of cortical bone histology to estimate age at death. In M. Y. İşcan (Ed.), *Age Markers in the Human Skeleton.* Springfield, IL: Charles C. Thomas, pp. 195–207.

Stout, S. D. (1992). Methods of determining age at death using bone microstructure. In S. R. Saunders and M. A. Katzenberg (Eds), *Skeletal Biology of Past Peoples: Research Methods.* New York: Wiley-Liss, pp. 21–35.

Suchey, J. M. (1979). Problems in the aging of females using the os pubis. *American Journal of Physical Anthropology* **51**: 467–470.

Suchey, J. M. (1987). Male pubic age determination—instructional casts. Typescript material distributed with Suchey–Brooks Male Instructional Casts. Bellvue, CO: France Casting.

Suchey, J. M., Wisely, D. V., Green R. F., and Noguchi, T. T. (1979). Analysis of dorsal pitting in the *os pubis* in an extensive sample of modern American females. *American Journal of Physical Anthropology* **51**: 517–540.

Suchey, J. M., Owens, P. A., Wisely, D.V., and Noguchi, T. T. (1984). Skeletal aging of unidentified persons. In T. A. Rathbun and J. E. Buikstra (Eds), *Human Identification: Case Studies in Forensic Anthropology*. Springfield, IL: Charles C. Thomas, pp. 278–297.

Suchey, J. M., Wisely, D. V., and Katz, D. (1986). Evaluation of the Todd and McKern–Stewart methods for aging the male *os pubis*. In K. J. Reichs (Ed.), *Forensic Osteology: Advances in the Identification of Human Remains*. Springfield, IL: Charles C. Thomas, pp. 33–67.

Suchey, J. M., Brooks, S. T., and Katz, D. (1988). Instructional materials accompanying female pubic symphyseal models of the Suchey–Brooks system. Bellvue, CO: France Casting.

Suslick, K. S. (1999). In his own words . . . UI chemist meets the federal district court. *Inside Illinois*, 15 April 1999, p. 7.

Sutherland, L. D., and Suchey, J. M. (1991). Use of the ventral arc in pubic sex determination. *Journal of Forensic Sciences* **36**: 501–511.

Symes, S. A., Berryman, H. E., and Smith, O. C. (1998). Saw marks in bone: introduction and examination of residual kerf contour. In K. J. Reichs (Ed.), *Forensic Osteology: Advances in the Identification of Human Remains*, 2nd edn. Springfield, IL: Charles C. Thomas, pp. 389–409.

Symes, S. A., Williams, J. A., Murray, E. A., Hoffman, J. M., Holland, T. D., Saul, J. M., Saul, F. P., and Pope, E. J. (2002). Taphonomic context of sharp-force trauma in suspected cases of human mutilation and dismemberment. In W. D. Haglund and M. H. Sorg (Eds), *Advances in Forensic Taphonomy: Method, Theory, and Archaeological Perspectives*. Boca Raton, FL: CRC Press, pp. 403–434.

Tague, R. G. (1988). Bone resorption of the pubis and preauricular area in humans and non-human animals. *American Journal of Physical Anthropology* **76**: 251–267.

Tanner, J. M., Whitehouse, R. H., Marshall, W. A., Healy, M. J. R., and Goldstein, H. (1975). *Assessment of skeletal Maturity and Prediction of Adult Height (TW2 Method)*. New York: Academic Press.

Thieme, F. P., and Schull, W. J. (1957). Sex determination from the skeleton. *Human Biology* **29**: 242–273.

Todd, T. W. (1920). Age changes in the pubic bone: 1, the male white pubis. *American Journal of Physical Anthropology* **3**: 286–334.

Todd, T. W., and Lyon, D.W. (1924). Endocranial suture closure: its progress and age relationship. Part I. Adult males of white stock. *American Journal of Physical Anthropology* **7**: 326–384.

Todd, T. W., and Lyon, D. W. (1925a). Cranial suture closure: its progress and age relationship. Part II. Ectocranial closure in adult males of white stock. *American Journal of Physical Anthropology* **8**: 23–45.

Todd, T. W., and Lyon, D. W. (1925b). Endocranial suture closure: its progress and age relationship. Part III. Adult males of Negro stock. *American Journal of Physical Anthropology* **8**: 47–71.

Todd, T. W., and Lyon, D. W. (1925c). Cranial suture closure: its progress and age relationship. Part IV. Ectocranial closure in adult males of Negro stock. *American Journal of Physical Anthropology* **8**: 149–168.

Trotter, M. (1970). Estimation of stature from intact long limb bones. In T. D. Stewart (Ed.), *Personal Identification in Mass Disasters.* Washington, DC: Smithsonian Institution Press, pp. 71–83.

Trotter, M., and Gleser, G. (1951). The effects of ageing on stature. *American Journal of Physical Anthropology* **9**: 311–324.

Trotter, M., and Gleser, G. C. (1952). Estimation of stature from long bones of American whites and Negroes. *American Journal of Physical Anthropology* **10**: 463–514.

Trotter, M., and Gleser, G. (1958). A re-evaluation of estimation of stature based on measurements of stature taken during life and of long bones after death. *American Journal of Physical Anthropology* **16**: 79–123.

Trotter, M., and Gleser, G. (1977). Corrigenda to "Estimation of stature from long limb bones of American whites and Negroes." *American Journal of Physical Anthropology* **47**: 355–356.

Tsokos, M., Schultz, F., and Pieschel, K. (1999). Unusual injury pattern in a case of post-mortem animal depredation by a domestic German shepherd. *American Journal of Forensic Medicine and Pathology* **20**: 247–250.

Ubelaker, D. H. (1984). Positive identification from the radiographic comparison of frontal sinus patterns. In T. A. Rathbun and J. E. Buikstra (Eds), *Human Identification: Case Studies in Forensic Anthropology.* Springfield, IL: Charles C. Thomas, pp. 399–411.

Ubelaker, D. H. (1989). *Human Skeletal Remains: Excavation, Analysis, Interpretation*, 2nd edn. Washington, DC: Taraxacum.

Ubelaker, D. H. (1992). Hyoid fracture and strangulation. *Journal of Forensic Sciences* **37**: 1216–1222.

Ubelaker, D. (1999). Dorsey, George Amos. In J. A. Garraty and M. C. Carnes (Eds), *American National Biography*, Vol. 6. New York: Oxford University Press, pp. 764–765.

Ubelaker, D. H. (2002). Approaches to the study of commingling in human skeletal biology. In W. D. Haglund and M. H. Sorg (Eds), *Advances in Forensic Taphonomy: Method, Theory, and Archaeological Perspectives.* Boca Raton, FL: CRC Press, pp. 331–351.

Ubelaker, D. H., and Volk, C. G. (2002). A test of the Phenice method for the estimation of sex. *Journal of Forensic Sciences* **47**: 19–24.

Vass, A. A., Bass, W. M., Wolt, J. D., Foss, J. E., and Ammons, J. T. (1992). Time since death determinations of human cadavers using soil solution. *Journal of Forensic Sciences* **37**: 1236–1253.

Walker, P. L. (1995). Problems of preservation and sexism in sexing: some lessons from historical collections for paleodemographers. In S. R. Saunders and A. Herring (Eds), *Grave Reflections, Portraying the Past Through Cemetery Studies.* Toronto: Canadian Scholar's Press, pp. 31–40.

Walker, P. L. (1997). Wife beating, boxing, and broken noses: skeletal evidence for the cultural patterning of violence. In D. Martin and D. Frayer (Eds), *Troubled Times: Violence and Warfare in the Past.* New York: Gordon and Breach, pp. 145–175.

Walker, R. A., and Lovejoy, C. (1985). Radiographic changes in the clavicle and proximal femur and their use in the determination of skeletal age at death. *American Journal of Physical Anthropology* **68**: 67–78.

Walker, P. L., Cook, D. C., and Lambert, P. M. (1997). Skeletal evidence for child abuse: a physical anthropological perspective. *Journal of Forensic Sciences* **42**: 196–207.

Wambaugh, J. (1989). *The Blooding.* New York: Bantam.

Warren, M. W., and Schultz, J. J. (2002). Post-cremation taphonomy and artifact preservation. *Journal of Forensic Sciences* **47**: 656–659.

Watson, A. (2000). A new breed of high-tech detectives. *Science* **289**: 850–854.

Washburn, S. L. (1948). Sex differences in the pubic bone. *American Journal of Physical Anthropology* **6**: 199–208.

Weaver, D. S. (1980). Sex differences in the ilia of a known sex and age sample of fetal and infant skeletons. *American Journal of Physical Anthropology* **52**: 191–195.

Weaver, D. S. (1998). Forensic aspects of fetal and neonatal skeletons. In K. J. Reichs, (Ed.), *Forensic Osteology: Advances in the Identification of Human Remains*, 2nd edn. Springfield, IL: Charles C. Thomas, pp. 187–203.

Webb, P. A. O., and Suchey, J. M. (1985). Epiphyseal union of the anterior iliac crest and medial clavicle in a modern multiracial sample of American males and females. *American Journal of Physical Anthropology* **68**: 457–466.

Weiss, E. (2004). Understanding muscle markers: lower limbs. *American Journal of Physical Anthropology* **125**: 232–238.

Weiss, K. M. (1972). On the systematic bias in skeletal sexing. *American Journal of Physical Anthropology* **37**: 239–250.

Wescott, D. J. (2005). Population variation in femur subtrochanteric shape. *Journal of Forensic Sciences* **50**: 286–293.

West, J. A., and Giles, E. (2001). Approaches to probable number of individuals (PNI) in extreme cases. *Proceedings of the American Academy of Forensic Sciences* **7**: 245 (abstract).

Whiting, W. C., and Zernicke, R. F. (1998). *Biomechanics of Musculoskeletal Injury.* Champaign, IL: Human Kinetics.

Willey, P., and Falsetti, T. (1991). Inaccuracy of height information of driver's licenses. *Journal of Forensic Sciences* **36**: 813–819.

Williams, R. A. (1991). Injuries in infants and small children resulting from witnesses and corroborated free falls. *Journal of Trauma-Injury, Infection and Critical Care* **31**: 1350–1352.

Wood, W. R., and Stanley, L. A. (1989). Recovery and identification of World War II dead: American graves registration activities in Europe. *Journal of Forensic Sciences* **34**: 1365–1373.

Yoder, C., Ubelaker, D. H., and Powell, J. F. (2001). Examination of variation in sternal rib end morphology relevant to age assessment. *Journal of Forensic Sciences* **46**: 223–227.

Young, J. Z. (1981). *The Life of Vertebrates*, 3rd edn. New York: Oxford University Press.

Zuo, Z-J., and Zhu, J-Z. (1991). Study on the microstructures of skull fracture. *Forensic Science International* **50**: 1–14.

INDEX